James A. Krisher

The Ongoing Work of Jesus

His Mission in Our Lives

TWENTY-THIRD PUBLICATIONS

185 Willow Street • PO BOX 180 • MYSTIC, CT 06355
TEL: 1-800-321-0411 • FAX: 1-800-572-0788
E-MAIL: ttpubs@aol.com • www.twentythirdpublications.com

Dedication

With profound gratitude,
I dedicate this book to my parents,
Jack and Doris Krisher,
whose immense love and generosity
have revealed to me the face of God.

The Scripture passages contained herein are from the *New Revised Standard Version of the Bible,* copyright ©1989, by the Division of Christian Education of the National Council of Churches of Christ in the U.S.A. All rights reserved.

Twenty-Third Publications
A Division of Bayard
185 Willow Street
P.O. Box 180
Mystic, CT 06355
(860) 536-2611
(800) 321-0411
www.twentythirdpublications.com

ISBN:1-58595-210-9
Library of Congress Catalog Card Number: 2002101731
Printed in the U.S.A.

Acknowledgments

I am deeply appreciative of the encouragement I have received from so many people as I worked on this book. I am particularly grateful to my assistant here at the Spiritual Renewal Center, Gary Thomas Smith, who read through every chapter as it was written—often several times over. He gave me valuable feedback on each chapter's content and offered helpful editorial suggestions from his experience as a journalist.

My wife, Debra, and my four children, Joseph, Benjamin, Elizabeth, and young James, were very patient with me when I seemed preoccupied with my writing, and so caring in their inquiries as to how I was doing and how the book was coming. I thank God for the blessings they bring to my life. My colleagues at the Center have also been most supportive, especially Sr. Marise May and Lana Riley, both of them valued members of our spiritual direction staff.

Many people have allowed me to share their stories with you through this book. Every story is true, although in every instance I have changed the name of the person whose story is being told. To each one of these brothers and sisters, I extend my thanks.

Contents

Introduction

On the wall of my office at the Spiritual Renewal Center, in a corner of the room reserved for spiritual direction sessions, there hangs a large and striking image of Jesus Christ. It's a copy of an icon that was painted in the sixth century. The original is in St. Catherine's Monastery at Mount Sinai, and it is among the most ancient representations of Christ in existence today.

Directees and visitors frequently comment on the icon. I enjoy telling them about its history, and pointing out how the artist has depicted in the face of Jesus the mystery of both his death and his resurrection. Depending on how you look at it, you can see either a man of suffering or the glorified Lord.

Of course, not everyone who sees the icon likes it. When it comes to religious art, everyone seems to have his or her own taste—a picture that speaks powerfully of Christ to one person may leave another person cold. Yet I've always been very fond of this icon myself, and I find my eyes drawn to it repeatedly during the day. When I'm in the middle of an appointment with someone, it reminds me of Christ's presence with us, loving us and guiding us. When I'm sitting at my desk or working on the computer, a quick glance toward that image more often than not becomes a lingering gaze, and a moment of prayer.

Throughout these two millennia, artists have been free to depict Jesus according to their own light, for the Bible gives no description of him at all. So one ancient catacomb painter can show him beardless, with cropped, curly hair, while most

Western artists have produced variations of the more familiar Jesus, with long brown hair and a beard. And all the different cultures of the earth have produced representations of the savior with the features of their own race. To imagine his face, and to contemplate his face as others have imagined it, has always been a spiritually nourishing practice for Christians. So perhaps we can count it a blessing that no one knows for sure what he actually looked like.

We can surmise, of course, that as a Palestinian Jew Jesus would no doubt have shared the physical characteristics of his people. And since he was a construction worker who spent his early adult years hefting stones for the walls of buildings, this carpenter from Nazareth would have likely been a very muscular guy, not the frail Jesus who appears in some of the more sentimental works of art.

But beyond this, we can say little. The evangelists didn't think the details of his height and hair and eye color were even worth noting. They were more concerned with conveying to us what his life was about. Indeed, what Jesus looked like is a mere curiosity, intriguing to ponder but ultimately of no importance whatsoever. What matters is who Jesus was, how he lived, and what he lived and died for—this is the stuff of substance for people of faith. This is what we seek to learn as we peer through the window of the Scriptures to observe his actions and savor his words, aware that this Jesus of the Bible is the same Jesus we know today and walk with daily.

Lately, in my own reading, I've found myself drawn again and again to those places in the gospels where Jesus speaks of his personal sense of mission. Over and over again, in a variety of ways, he expresses his deeply felt convictions regarding his purpose on earth, what he was meant to be about in his life and what he was *not* meant to be about. Some of these statements can be quite surprising, even shocking.

These "mission statements" of Jesus are the basis for this book. I've selected a number of them, and have dedicated a chapter to each one. I look first at the saying in its biblical context, then seek to explore what it might mean in terms of Jesus' ongoing mission both in our lives as well as in the world today. I also consider what it might mean for us to be collaborators with Jesus—not just recipients, but sharers in his mission.

As a teacher of the New Testament, I am well aware of the questions regarding the historicity of specific gospel texts, and the many factors that influenced the transmission of the gospel in those earliest decades of Christianity. But this is not an academic study. I approach the texts I've selected as representative of the "sort of thing" that Jesus said—as sayings that at least reflect the mind of Jesus even if we can't know his exact words. I have listened to them as the living word of a living Jesus and I have prayed with them, and this book is the fruit of that listening.

The opening chapter serves as a foundation for what follows. It underlines the fundamental truth of the resurrection, and the reality of Jesus as not just a historical figure of the past but a living presence in our lives. I also look at what it means to live in relationship with him on a day-to-day basis. Chapter two focuses on the concept of mission, and how each of us is guided in life by a sense of mission even when we've never thought about it that way or tried to articulate it. Jesus too was guided by a sense of mission, and each of the remaining chapters explores a different aspect of this guiding mission of Christ.

The writing of this book is a labor of my love for Jesus, and I trust that my desire to honor him with my words pleases him in some small way. He knows well how much resistance I have had to overcome to get the job done, and how persistently he has had to nudge me back to this project, which I more than once abandoned. It is my fervent hope that this book might lead you to a richer understanding of Jesus, a greater appreciation of his love for you, and a keener sensitivity to his presence and activity in your day-to-day life.

One

Living with a Living Lord

Whenever God's grace touches a human life, all human lives are somehow enriched. Whenever God's call is received and embraced, the universe is changed and the course of history redirected. This is true in every instance, however hidden or seemingly insignificant the recipient of divine favor may be. Every age has countless anonymous souls whose secret intimacy with God subtly molds the future of humanity. Through their prayer, their compassionate interaction with others, and their hidden acts of virtue, love's liberating power becomes more available for others.

Yet every age has its great luminaries as well—saintly men and women whose relationship with the Creator has a more public and dramatic impact both on their own time and on succeeding generations. Paul of Tarsus was such a saint.

Paul was in his early thirties when he met Jesus, a man he thought was dead. Oddly enough, it happened while he was "ravaging the church" (Acts 8:3), an activity he'd undertaken not out of wickedness but out of sincere devotion to his faith.

Indeed, Paul had always been exceptionally devoted to his faith; he was, in his own words, "advanced in Judaism beyond many among my people of the same age, for I was far more zealous for the traditions of my ancestors" (Gal 1:14). From his religious perspective, those sectarians who called themselves "followers of the Way" were in fact followers of a false prophet—hadn't the Nazarene been so judged by the leaders in Jerusalem? Paul was determined to stop the spread of their movement, and so after witnessing the stoning of Stephen in Jerusalem, he headed off to Damascus to arrest any Christians he might find there (Acts 7:55—8:1, 9:1-2). That's when it happened. Paul tells us:

> While I was on my way and approaching Damascus, about noon a great light from heaven suddenly shone about me. I fell to the ground and heard a voice saying to me, "Saul, Saul, why are you persecuting me?" I answered, "Who are you, Lord?" Then he said to me, "I am Jesus of Nazareth whom you are persecuting."…I asked, "What am I to do, Lord?" The Lord said to me, "Get up and go to Damascus; there you will be told everything that has been assigned to you to do." (Acts 22:6-8, 10)

Paul, enemy of the Christians, had suddenly found himself face to face with their Lord. How shocked he must have been to encounter Jesus alive when he knew the man had been executed and sealed in a tomb! What a blow to his worldview, what an upset to his thinking!

He must have felt mortified, like a man who slanders another, then turns to see him standing at the door, hearing all. He must have felt afraid, as fear grips a guilty person about to be sentenced. He must have felt like Isaiah in the temple, filled with his own uncleanness in the presence of the Holy (Isa 6:5). Yet, like Isaiah, Paul was cleansed, forgiven, accepted. A stunned Paul experienced the love of the living Jesus Christ, and his heart was captured forever.

The magnitude of this man's transformation redounds through history. What other moment of conversion has in turn led to so many other conversions across centuries, even millennia? Who else has provided so much challenge, so much inspiration, so much exhilarating truth as Paul has through his writings? It's true, he can at times be irritating as we listen to him with our modern, Western ears—he can strike us as arrogant, belligerent, stubborn. Ah, but such passion for Jesus! Here lies his holiness, despite his human foibles. Here lies the strength of his testimony, potent still after two thousand years.

On that Damascus road, as has often been said, Paul was converted to Christ, not to Christianity. This distinction is vital. No one sat down with Paul and convinced him by reasoned argument to join the growing Christian movement. Nor was he swayed because he heard dynamic preaching that moved him to accept Christian claims. No, Paul's conversion was not to a religion but to a person. Paul met someone—Jesus Christ—and he fell in love with that person and dedicated his life to him.

From that day forward, Paul testified unceasingly to the reality of the Risen Lord—and he insisted that he be heard not simply as another believer but as an eyewitness. "Have I not seen Jesus our Lord?" he exclaims in a letter to Corinth (1 Cor 9:1). And later in that same letter, Paul adds himself to an early Christian creed that listed witnesses to the Resurrected One. Putting himself in the esteemed company of Cephas and the Twelve, he declares "Last of all, as to one untimely born, he appeared also to me" (1 Cor 15:8). This claim ranks among the most direct testimonies to the resurrection in all of the New Testament. Here is a man speaking from firsthand experience:

"I saw him myself!" Paul says. "I know he's alive because I met him myself!" And there is no indication that he ever doubted the reality of what happened to him on that journey to Damascus.

In another letter, his epistle to the Philippians (3:5–15), this persecutor-turned-preacher tells of how the encounter with Jesus changed his outlook on everything. Earlier in his life, Paul had taken great pride in the fact that he was "a member of the people of Israel, of the tribe of Benjamin, a Hebrew born of Hebrews." He describes himself in his "before Christ" days as a zealous and righteous man according to the standards of his Pharisaic religion. "Yet," he writes, "these I have come to regard as loss because of Christ. More than that, I regard everything as loss because of the surpassing value of knowing Christ Jesus my Lord. For his sake I have suffered the loss of all things, and I regard them as rubbish, in order that I may gain Christ and be found in him."

Using bookkeeping metaphors, Paul here draws up his columns of assets and losses, and declares unequivocally that all those religious assets he once valued seem to be as so much "rubbish" in comparison to Christ. (The actual term Paul uses might more accurately be rendered as "manure.") Notice he does not say that he regards them as loss because of the surpassing value of his new church affiliation. He does not say that he suffered the loss of all things for the sake of his doctrinal stance, nor does he say that his hope is to gain stature in the eyes of his community. Such abstractions were not the first love of his heart. No, Paul's dedication was not primarily to a religion but to a relationship. It is for Jesus that he suffers loss. It is the surpassing value of knowing Christ personally that motivates his life, and it is gaining Christ that is his hope and goal.

Didn't Paul value his community of faith? Of course! Few

have written as eloquently as Paul on the need for solidarity with the people of God. Didn't he have strong doctrinal convictions? Of course—and no one can accuse him of soft-pedaling them either! But if these things were important to him, it was because he loved Christ. His relationship with Jesus was primary—it was the hub of the wheel, the foundation of the building, the heart of it all.

And Paul does not hesitate to set this as the standard for every Christian. Writing with all the authority of the Word of God, he says: "Let those of us then who are mature be of the same mind; and if you think differently about anything, this too God will reveal to you" (Phil 3:15). He says: "Brothers and sisters, join in imitating me, and observe those who live according to the example you have in us" (Phil 3:17). The great apostle holds forth his own spirituality as a model for believers of every age. As he avowed "the surpassing value of knowing Christ Jesus," so every believer is likewise to treasure relationship with Jesus above all else. According to Paul, to be a Christian is to be rooted in Christ, centered on Christ, and reaching toward Christ. According to Paul, to be a Christian is to live a life of personal commitment to the person of the risen Lord.

Many generations have come and gone since those pristine days when Paul lived and ministered. His seed faith and that of the other early missionaries has grown into a worldwide religion, embodied in diverse church families. And while some might bemoan the institutionalization of that early Christian fire, the institutions of Christianity have managed to preserve that fire (albeit in spite of themselves) through often hostile centuries to our own day. For the vitality of Christianity has always been the vitality of its Lord. While it's true that every era has stories of stupidity and abuse in the name of Jesus, every era has stories of changed lives too—men, women, and children who through the witness of the church met the living Christ, and like the apostle Paul, would never be the same again. Our own era is no different.

An encounter with the living Jesus

Jeremy encountered Jesus at age nineteen. He was struggling through his first year away from home at a major university, trying to cope with the loneliness, the pressure, and the suicide of another freshman on his dormitory floor. A Jesuit in the chaplaincy office suggested he check out a prayer group that met at a rectory in the city, and so Jeremy, figuring he had nothing to lose, went to his appointment with grace.

> At first I thought all those people in the room were crazy—they were talking to Jesus as if he were really there! I couldn't wait to get out of there. I joked about them all week long. Still, I went back the next Saturday night, and that's when it happened. About halfway through the meeting I had an overwhelming sense of Christ's presence surrounding me and filling me. I found myself saying over and over in my head: It's really true! He's really here! He's really alive! I started smiling and smiling, and I couldn't stop smiling for weeks—the muscles in my face hurt from smiling, but I was so filled with joy!

Jeremy still smiles with joy when he tells of it—he's so in love with Jesus, now nearly thirty years later.

Noreen was at mid-life when her husband left her, and she had to live through an unwanted and painful divorce. In the months that followed, she slipped into depression as she faced the prospect of life alone. When she was invited to attend a women's retreat offered by her Lutheran church, she quickly accepted, never dreaming of what that retreat would bring to her.

One evening, I sat listening to other women tell of their relationship with Jesus, and the deep peace that it brought to them. I had always gone to church, but I had never experienced Christ as a reality in my life. Later that same night I went to the chapel, and fell on my knees before a picture of the Lord. I told him how much I wanted to know him; I prayed earnestly for him to reveal himself to me. He answered my prayer! All at once, I had a powerful awareness of him right there, looking at me with great love and compassion. I sensed him saying "I am with you always." When I returned from retreat, I was a changed person—the depression had disappeared! I was filled with new hope for the future, a hope that was based on the presence of Jesus in my life.

Noreen has long enjoyed that presence, and has even served as a missionary in Africa. Many times over, she says, Jesus has reminded her of his fidelity with those same words: I am with you always.

Jeremy and Noreen tell of how their encounter with a living Jesus was a surprise—completely unexpected, just as it was for St. Paul. While both of them had been raised in churches, and heard often of the resurrection, they had never grasped its full meaning. Jeremy says,

I guess I thought of the resurrection as an assurance to those early disciples that Jesus was in heaven, and an assurance to us that we would meet him someday when we died. But it never occurred to me that he was still around, that I could meet him now, and that he could be active in my life here.

Others have reported that, prior to actually meeting Christ, they thought Christianity meant following the teachings of a great but dead holy man, or honoring the memory of a wise religious founder long since gone.

But Jesus is not dead. He is not gone. He is risen, and he remains among us even today as "the pioneer and perfecter of our faith" (Heb 12:2), as "the head of the body, the church" (Col 1:18). And as Thomas à Kempis writes in his book, *Imitation of Christ*, "The person who finds Jesus finds a good treasure—indeed, a good beyond all good…it is wealth to live with him."

To live with Jesus Christ is to enter the realm of mystery, for he exists on a different plane of reality, not subject to the rules of space and time. We cannot perceive him with our bodily senses; we cannot embrace him or read his mood as we might read others from the clues of facial expression or body language. Relating to Jesus requires the cultivation of our spiritual senses—we must learn how to listen for him with our heart, and how to see him with the inner eye of love.

Often this requires practice, even a lifetime of developing spiritual sensitivity, as not many are instantly adept at it. But Jesus himself works with us, helping to open those channels of communion that will make possible a deepened intimacy. And if impatience with our own slow progress should discourage or burden our hearts, we need only remember that he is more eager than we are, and he has both the desire and the means to complete what he has begun in us (see Phil 1:6).

If living with Christ has its undeniable distinctiveness, it is also in many ways similar to living with any other person. Little by little we become familiar with his ways, as we would with a spouse or roommate or close friend, even to the point where we might anticipate what he wants in many instances. Yet at the same time, because he is a free being, there always remains an element of unpredictability in our relationship with him. We do best not to assume that we know his mind when facing a new situation or a changed circumstance. As Paul twice reminds his readers, "For who has known the mind of the Lord? Or who has been his counselor?" (Rom 11:34; 1 Cor 2:16). Even as we would respectfully consult with a friend to ascertain or confirm her thoughts on a given matter, so we do the same with the risen Jesus. And as his place in our lives is pre-eminent, we often will seek his guidance in prayer.

In times of trouble or when we're feeling down, the comfort and assistance of those who love us is invaluable—and Jesus offers this to us as no one else can. He knows our trials as well as we do because he knows them within us, and he loves us more than we love ourselves. This is one of the most frequently cited blessings of knowing Christ—the strong, affirming support of the Savior that gives peace in the midst of difficulty. So often from the lips of Christians come exclamations like these: "I would never have made it without him!" "It's Jesus who got me through it!" Truly, whether we're dealing with "hardship, or distress, or persecution, or famine, or nakedness, or peril, or sword...in all these things we are more than conquerors through him who loved us" (Rom 8:35, 37).

But while people who love us give comfort, they can be major irritants as well, especially when because of that love they challenge our complacency or disrupt our sense of peace. Jesus is really good at that too—and once again he can do it as no one else can, for he is not deceived by the excuses we use to deceive even ourselves. He won't be fooled by our masks of innocence or deterred by our whining or discouraged by our apathy. Because he is so fiercely dedicated to us, he can be relentless in calling us to conversion. As he makes clear through the seer John, "I reprove and discipline those whom I love" (Rev 3:19). So living with Christ is not always relaxing.

In any relationship, whether it be a marriage, a friendship, or even a business connection, we must be willing to give time and attention to the other, or the bond between us weakens and we drift apart. Our relationship with Jesus is no different. We need to continually choose to give him our time and attention.

Of course, in reality we are never apart from Jesus, but in our minds and hearts we can be unavailable to him. We can let the busyness of the day so consume us that there remains nothing left to give to him. We can let "the cares of the world, and the lure of wealth, and the desire for other things" choke off our hunger for Jesus (see Mark 4:19).

And strange as it may seem, it's even possible for religion itself to distract us from the Lord. We can get so preoccupied with our pious routines, with what Baron von Hügel called "all the little churchinesses," that maintaining these routines becomes our dedication, and we no longer listen for the voice of Jesus. Or we can become so focused on our denomination-al loyalties, or on zeal for "keeping the rules" (and making sure that others keep them!) that we lose sight of the living Jesus, who beckons to us. In the final analysis, it matters not what has aroused our fervor—if it diverts us from contact with Christ the result is the same: diminished intimacy, drifting desire.

Whenever we begin to live with someone else, we are intro-duced into a whole new circle of relationships. Our new spouse or friend comes with family connections and a com-munity of acquaintances we might never have otherwise met, but who now become part of our life together. To live with the living Lord likewise brings us into a new circle of relationships, a community of those who serve Christ that is broader and more inclusive than any other community on earth. And just as we cannot claim to love our spouse while despising those our spouse has loved, so we cannot claim to love the Lord without loving all who belong to him. Not for long can we insulate ourselves in a cozy corner with Jesus, for he always comes with a crowd. Closeness with him inevitably binds us to all who believe—those on earth and those in heaven.

What a grand communion of saints we are! Here and now, we are one with the likes of the great St. Paul, and with holy men and women and children of every age, "from every nation, from all tribes and peoples and languages" (Rev 7:9). Here and now, through the risen Christ flows that uncreated energy that transforms souls and shapes our common future. No earthly fortune can compare to "the boundless riches of Christ" (Eph 3:8), to the surpassing value of knowing him.

Nothing ever could. Nothing ever will.

Questions for reflection

1. The book opens by emphasizing the spiritual interconnectedness of the human family. Can you think of instances in your own experience when God's grace given to another person has been a blessing to you as well? Can you think of a specific grace that you received that has served to bless others too?

2. "Paul's dedication was not primarily to a religion but to a relationship." What do you think is the difference, if any, between being dedicated to Christianity and being dedicated to Christ? Do you think it's possible to be equally dedicated to both? Whom do you know who exemplifies the priorities and commitment of Paul? What would you see as indicators that someone is more concerned with the religion than with the relationship?

3. Jeremy and Noreen had unexpected and powerful encounters with the living Christ. In what ways do you connect with their experiences? Do you have an experience of encountering Christ that you could share with others?

4. Sometimes people relate to Jesus as if he were remote and hard to contact, or as if his affection must be won. How does it change the practice of Christian faith when we understand that "he is more eager than we are" to have a deeper communion with us?

5. "But while people who love us give comfort, they can be major irritants as well, especially when because of that love they challenge our complacency or disrupt our sense of peace." Have you ever found Jesus to be irritating or disruptive or relentless in calling you to conversion? What were some of the occasions when Christ disrupted your sense of peace?

Two

A Sense of Mission

People were astonished when Barry announced that he was leaving his government job. Why would a bright young man walk out of a high-paying, influential position to run a food program for poor and homeless people? Why would this West Point graduate with a master's degree in public administration step off the upward track and take such a huge cut in pay and prestige? No one could understand it—not even Barry himself. He says,

> Whenever someone asked me why, I'd find myself struggling for an answer, I knew it didn't make any sense, and I could come up with no rational explanation for what I was doing. I just knew I needed to do it—I felt called—and that's what I'd tell people. Often I'd get blank stares, and an uneasy silence would follow. And then we'd talk about the weather—it was a much more comfortable topic of conversation!

The questions didn't end, even after he started his new position. But his own self-questioning was the most persistent.

> I kept asking myself: What am I doing? Have I made the

biggest mistake of my life? I was feeling so much fear in those first six months. It would wake me up at night and fill me as I drove to work. But when I was there working at my desk or talking to one of the guests, I found a comfort deep down within myself. Somehow what I was doing felt right, and I knew I needed to stay the course.

Barry has a sense of mission.

Eduardo finished college with a degree in religion, convinced that he had a vocation to a life of ministry. His plans were to work for a few years in a parish, and then go back to school for a graduate degree in theology. He also hoped to meet "the right woman" and get married—which of course ruled out ordination to priesthood in the Catholic Church. But that was okay with him. He believed he was called to ministry and marriage, and that God would make it possible for him to live that call.

Eduardo gave himself wholeheartedly to serving his parishioners, finding great joy and fulfillment in it. Yet he was bewildered to find himself being urged on every side to enter the seminary and become a priest. Before long he began to question his own discernment, and finally he decided to apply for admission to a religious order. Eduardo says:

> I wanted to do whatever God wanted of me, and I guess I thought maybe God was speaking to me through these other people. So I applied and was accepted. Then, about two weeks before I was to enter the novitiate, I went on a retreat weekend. I spent considerable time alone in the chapel that first evening, giving myself over to God and rededicating myself to God. I went to bed at peace, yet with a strange feeling of melancholy.

Eduardo tells the next part of his story with a great intensity of feeling.

I wish I could find words to express what happened to me during that night. I can only say that God touched me. I "heard" nothing, but the communication was clear. God told me that I was right about my call at the beginning, and that I shouldn't let other people steer me. God told me that I already was who he wanted me to be, and that I didn't have to become anything else to serve him. I got up the next morning absolutely certain that I was meant to be a married minister. Needless to say, I didn't enter the novitiate. I never felt such great freedom of heart, such joy and love for God as I felt in the aftermath of that experience.

Eduardo continues to minister full-time in the Catholic Church, now as a married man and the father of several children. His vocation hasn't always been easy, but he never again questioned its rightness for him. "I know I'm living as God intends me to live," he says. "It's like I was created to walk this path."

Eduardo has a sense of mission.

Not everyone has such a strong, clearly felt sense of mission as Barry and Eduardo. But most of us have at least some awareness of what we're meant to be about in life, what our vocation is, what it includes, and what it doesn't. For many people, this sense of mission is focused heavily on family—parents, spouse, children—and often includes a particular life work.

People who choose careers in teaching or medicine or ministry often have a highly developed sense of mission, but we might just as likely find it in clerical workers or musicians or farmers. A builder once told me, "My grandfather was a carpenter, my father was a carpenter, and I'm a carpenter too. It's a talent I have and I love to share it. It's what I'm called to give to the world." A prison guard nearing retirement expressed how there were times when she hated going in to work, and she'd toyed with the idea of leaving the job. But she knew that working at the prison was her mission in life, that her integrity and compassion could make a difference there. She had no regrets at all.

In addition to family and career, there are other interests that may manifest a sense of mission. For example, Mary works tirelessly in her spare time to raise funds for the local symphony, while Jake belongs to several environmental organizations and is deeply dedicated to ecological concerns. Trina spends her free time making phone calls for a local peace and justice organization. And Michael volunteers as a sports coach for youth athletic programs. If you talk to any one of them you quickly become aware of the passion that motivates such self-giving. In each case, this passion has a very specific goal. If you ask them why they've chosen this cause and not another, they'll explain that their project just seems to fit them; it expresses something of who they are.

A sense of mission, then, can encompass many dimensions of a person's life. Even if we haven't yet attempted to articulate our own sense of mission, or find it difficult to do so, it remains active within us nevertheless, influencing our choices of lifestyle, career, leisure pursuits, and so on. It's that "something deeper" that moves us down a particular course, sometimes in spite of our reasoned resistance. It's that determination to see a work through that relativizes other endeavors. So strong is this determination in some people that they willingly suffer privation and loss to accomplish what they feel they've been called to do. Their mission is of such great importance to them that their physical well-being and even life itself become secondary concerns.

Faithfulness to our mission

Our sense of mission is integral to our identity as God created us; it's rooted in who we are as unique individuals. So, the question "What am I to do?" is inseparable from the question "Who am I?" The answer to both questions can only be found in the depths of our own souls, where we discover that word of God which is personally addressed to each one of us. For indeed,

> It is not in heaven, that you should say, "Who will go up to heaven for us, and get it for us so that we may hear it and observe it?" Neither is it beyond the sea, that you should say, "Who will cross to the other side of the sea for us, and get it for us so that we may hear it and observe it?" No, the word is very near to you; it is in your mouth and in your heart for you to observe. (Deut 30:12–14)

This is why when we're faithful to our mission we feel authentic, true to ourselves. We experience coherence between our outward life and our inward reality. We're somehow conscious that we're doing what we're meant to do, being who we're meant to be. In some individuals, this feeling is so strong that they cannot even imagine themselves pursuing any other course in life than the one they have chosen. Barry expressed how he "needed to do it"; it "felt right." Eduardo said he was "created to walk this path."

Likewise, we might question if we're off track in our lives when we experience dissonance between who we are and what we're about. We may become aware that we aren't "cut out" for something, even when it's very appealing to us on other levels. This dissonance is often expressed with phrases like "That job just wasn't me," or "I never felt at home with that," or "For some reason, it doesn't sit right with me."

Our sense of mission enables us—even requires us—to prioritize all our varied interests in life. So, for example, if my mission includes parenthood, there are many other good things to which I may have to say no. I may choose not to take a job that requires being away from home for weeks at a time, even though that position is very appealing and worthwhile. In the same way, if I have a sense of call to work with Habitat for Humanity, I may very well have to say no to an invitation to lead a scout troop. Thus in the course of my life, there will be lots of good things I will not do so that I can focus my energies on what I'm meant to do. People who don't prioritize according to their sense of mission inevitably become scattered, moving in too many different directions and accomplishing very little.

Organizations realize this as well. Many corporations and associations and ministries and churches have put time and effort into articulating a mission statement to guide the functioning of their group. The process of formulating a mission statement can be tedious, as it requires a group to express not only what they do but also who they are as an organization. The inevitable haggling over the words to be used becomes a vital part of the process of self-definition. Once a mission statement is arrived at, it becomes a useful touchstone in future decision making. The group can ask: is this work within our mission focus? Will this project take us too far afield?

Our friend St. Paul further illustrates these points. After his encounter with Jesus on the road to Damascus, Paul worked with steady zeal to preach Jesus Christ to the Gentiles, convinced that this was his specific calling—indeed, that it was his life's purpose from the beginning. "God, who had set me apart before I was born and called me through his grace," Paul writes, "was pleased to reveal his Son to me, so that I might proclaim him among the Gentiles" (Gal 1:15–16). Elsewhere he explains "this grace was given to me to bring to the Gentiles the news of the boundless riches of Christ" (Eph 3:8).

Because he had this particular mission, there were other things Paul would not do—not because they weren't good things but because he wasn't meant to do them. He obviously did not feel called to settle down and pastor churches long-term, as evidenced by his widespread travels through the ancient world, constantly moving from city to city. Rather, he understood that he was to be a church planter, someone who laid foundations. Others could do the watering and the building (see 1 Cor 3:6–10). And since his vocation was preaching, he readily left administering baptism to others (with few exceptions). "Christ did not send me to baptize but to proclaim the gospel," he writes in 1 Corinthians 1:17.

So strong was Paul's sense of mission that, like some of the prophets of old, he experienced it as an irresistible drive within him. "If I proclaim the gospel, this gives me no ground for boasting, for an obligation is laid on me, and woe to me if I do not proclaim the gospel!" (1 Cor 9:16). He could no more stop preaching than he could stop being Paul!

In living out his mission Paul faced adversity of every kind, "insults, hardships, persecutions, and calamities for the sake of Christ" (2 Cor 12:10). Yet nothing could deter him from doing what he needed to do. Out of love for the living Jesus, Paul was dragged before religious leaders and political authorities alike, never cowering in their presence but speaking boldly of what he knew. When he finally reached Rome—his missionary goal of many years—it was only as a prisoner. Tradition has it that he was martyred during the reign of the emperor Nero. Faithfully, Paul had carried out his mission to the end—just like his Lord.

Jesus embraces his mission

Jesus of Nazareth lived with a profound sense of mission. This might seem to be an entirely self-evident truth, as Christians recognize Jesus as the incarnation of the eternal word of God, the second person of the Trinity who came into the world to accomplish our salvation. Over and over again, the New Testament tells us that he came because he was sent by the Father—in John's gospel alone, this point is made forty times! He was here because he had a mission; surely, his mission awareness must have powerfully guided his words and deeds.

Yet Christian faith also recognizes that Jesus was fully human, and as the early church councils taught, he is like us in all things except sin. He experienced the full gamut of human emotions, as well as sexual feelings and attractions, uncertainties, pain, and confusion. He was "one who in every respect has been tested as we are, yet without sin" (Heb 4:15). So though his identity and calling are unique in all of history, his human experience of self-discovery and of having a mission in life would be very much like our own. Like us, the man Jesus had to learn things gradually, as he "increased in wisdom and in years, and in divine and human favor" (Luke 2:52). Like us, he had to discover his path in life, and find ways to understand and live out that profound sense of mission.

It's not unusual for people to catch glimmers of their life's purpose even in childhood. A medical student reports "I think I set my sights on being a doctor when I was seven." A minister says "Somehow even as a kid I always knew I'd end up a pastor." The gospels indicate that this was the case for Jesus as well. The very first words attributed to him in the gospel of Luke speak of his awareness, even in adolescence, that his life had an overriding purpose that he could not ignore.

After a family journey to Jerusalem, Jesus deliberately stays behind in the city, and his frantic parents spend days searching for him. No doubt they imagined all kinds of terrible explanations for the disappearance of their only son. What a mixture of relief and consternation must have filled Mary and Joseph when they found him in the temple, listening to the teachers and asking them questions! As they grasp that he was never really "lost" but had remained there by choice, Mary exclaims "Why have you treated us like this?" The twelve-year-old's reply is puzzling to his mother and father, but reveals his budding sense of call. "He said to them, 'Why were you searching for me? Did you not know that I must be in my Father's house?'" (Luke 2:49).

When next we meet him in the gospels, it is at the river Jordan where he is baptized by the charismatic preacher John. There Jesus has a powerful religious experience that deepens his realization of his identity and call. "And just as he was coming up out of the water, he saw the heavens torn apart and the Spirit descending like a dove on him. And a voice came from heaven, 'You are my Son, the Beloved; with you I am well pleased'" (Mark 1:10–11). This event marked for Jesus the end of his years as a carpenter, and the beginning of his major "lifework."

Such a watershed event in anyone's life is never forgotten; it remains in consciousness as an energizing memory, ever fresh despite the passage of time. Once you've had such an experience, you can never tell your life's story without including it, and you can never be fully understood apart from it. When the path forward grows obscure, or self-doubt plagues the mind, recalling such formative moments of insight and clarity can bring renewed vision and confidence. Surely Jesus cherished the memory of his baptism, and shared it with those who were close to him, and returned to it often to be renewed when he felt discouraged or uncertain.

Following this experience, the gospels tell us that Jesus spent time alone in the wilderness. It's almost as if he needed to process the full implications of what he'd experienced at the Jordan, and work out prayerfully within himself the specific shape that his mission was to take. There were many possibilities that confronted him, and clearly they were not all consistent with who he was and what he was called to do. Satan was averse to the accomplishment of his mission, and tested him with many seductive suggestions. For Jesus at that point, there was no doubting the big picture—he was the Son of God on a mission to save. But the devil was in the details.

St. Ignatius of Loyola, in his *Spiritual Exercises*, speaks of temptation as a common aftermath of a peak religious experience in a person's life. He writes:

> Often during this later period we ourselves act either through our own reasoning...or through the influence of either a good or an evil spirit. In this way we form various projects and convictions which are not coming immediately from God our Lord. Hence these need to be very carefully examined before they are fully accepted or carried into effect.

The desert was where Jesus did this careful examining, rejecting the allurements of Satan. The desert was where Jesus' own sense of mission was refined for action. When he returns to Galilee, he appears as a man who knows what he is about, boldly proclaiming his good news.

Initially, it seems, his work met with great success—he was the proverbial "big fish in the small bowl" of Capernaum and the surrounding countryside. He made quite a splash with his preaching, his exorcisms, and his healings. His rapidly spreading reputation brought mobs of sick and suffering people eager for a cure. And so Jesus was faced with the first big decision regarding the priorities of his mission.

Mark tells us how, after a day of many healings, Jesus got up long before the sun and went off for some solitude and prayer. When Simon and his companions found him, they urged him to return, "'Everyone is searching for you.' He answered, 'Let us go on to the neighboring towns, so that I may proclaim the message there also; for that is what I came out to do'" (Mark 1:37–38).

And Jesus left town. No doubt there were still people unhealed, possessed, dissatisfied. But Jesus left town anyway. He had discerned that preaching the word of God to as many as possible must come first for him. His ministry could not be governed by other people's expectations or desires. His own sense of mission, so integral to his identity as Word of God— this alone would steer his course to the end of his earthly days, and beyond. His own sense of mission, alive and burning in his heart—this alone would define the contours of his ongoing work as Savior.

We now turn to a closer examination of the mission of Jesus as he perceived it, lived it, and lives it now.

Questions for Reflection

1. Barry and Eduardo are individuals with a strong sense of mission. Who do you know personally who exemplifies this? Would you say that you have a strong sense of mission? What does your mission in life include?

2. "Likewise, we might question if we're off track in our lives when we experience dissonance between who we are and what we're about." Have you ever experienced this kind of dissonance? When have you found yourself feeling that you weren't "cut out" for something you were involved in? Do you think such feelings always mean that you're not being true to your mission? What do you think would be the result if a person ignored these feelings and kept on the same path?

3. When Christians gather to talk about Jesus, questions often arise regarding whether or not he knew he was God, and how much he knew. In this chapter we read: "Like us, the man Jesus had to learn things gradually....Like us, he had to discover his path in life, and find ways to understand and live out that profound sense of mission." Do you agree? What are your thoughts on this subject?

4. "It's not unusual for people to catch glimmers of their life's purpose even in childhood." Were there any clues in your childhood indicating what your life's mission would be? Have you any stories, about yourself or someone close to you, that illustrate these childhood intuitions of God's call?

5. The chapter talks about how our sense of mission requires us to prioritize, to say no to some good things in order to keep focused on what we're meant to do. The chapter concludes by pointing to an instance in Jesus' life that demonstrates that prioritizing process. How has this happened in your own life? What happens when we can't or won't say no on occasion?

Three

A Mission
to Sinners

Readers familiar with Charlotte Brontë's great novel *Jane Eyre*
may remember a heartrending scene from early in Jane's life.
When she is still a young girl attending a Christian boarding
school in England, Jane is cruelly humiliated before her class-
mates by the imperious and self-righteous schoolmaster, Mr.
Brocklehurst. He calls Jane to the front of the class, and makes
her stand on a stool to be denounced as a liar. "You must be
on your guard against her," Brocklehurst exhorts the other children, "avoid her company, exclude her from your sports and
shut her out from your converse." He reasons that association
with a perceived sinner like Jane might contaminate the other
children. He assumes that the shunning of sinners is a duty of
Christian piety.

In fact, the child he so brutally accuses is innocent of wrongdoing. But the greater sadness in the scene is the absolute trav-
esty of Christianity that Mr. Brocklehurst represents. His "shun
the sinner" attitude could not be further from the example of
Jesus himself. Yet people like Mr. Brocklehurst can be found

throughout Christian history, and continue to fill more than one pew and pulpit in our churches today.

At the time of Jesus there were many who might be identified as "sinners" by different groups within Judaism, and treated as outcasts from "good" society. Most obviously there were those who openly flaunted the religious teachings of Jewish Law—prostitutes, thieves, and so on. Tax collectors were also viewed as sinners, dishonest and greedy. They were hated for their work in collecting monies for the unpopular King Herod, who collaborated with the Roman oppressors. Gentile people in general, pagans without the Law, might be considered sinners, as well as Jews who didn't practice their faith according to the strict standards of a particular religious leader or Jewish sect. Even a physical illness or deformity might mark someone as a sinner who is being punished by God, as is the case with the blind man in chapter nine of John's gospel. In that same chapter, Jesus himself is called a sinner for his perceived violation of Sabbath regulations.

It was presumed that no truly religious person would associate with sinners. The Scriptures themselves reflect this: "I do not sit with the worthless, nor do I consort with hypocrites; I hate the company of evildoers, and will not sit with the wicked," says the author of Psalm 26 (vv 4–5). Likewise, the writer of Psalm 139 prays, "Do I not hate those who hate you, O Lord? And do I not loathe those who rise up against you? I hate them with perfect hatred; I count them my enemies" (vv 21–22). Scorn for sinners was almost a mark of true devotion to God.

Apparently Jesus did not think this way. He sat with those deemed worthless and wicked, and welcomed the company of those considered to be evildoers. He did not hate the religious outcasts but loved them, and actually went out of his way to associate with them. He invited himself to stay at a known sinner's house while on a preaching tour (Luke 19:1–10). He initiated a conversation with a Samaritan woman, one whose marital status was highly suspect (John 4:1–27). He let a woman widely known to be a sinner approach and actually touch him, kissing his feet (Luke 7:36–50). And perhaps most scandalous of all, he shared meals with sinners; he broke bread with those who were judged unrighteous. Is it any wonder that he earned the reputation as a friend of "tax collectors and sinners"? (Matt 9:11).

Jesus' behavior toward sinners was not motivated by some vacuous need to rebel against authority or to draw attention to himself. Nor was he rejecting Jewish moral teaching or approving anyone's sinful conduct—on the contrary, he was ever calling people to repentance. But he did not wait until people were repentant before he and his disciples associated with them. He knew the expansiveness of the divine mercy, and knew that his human life must ever reveal that mercy. So seeking out and befriending sinners was clearly part of his mission on earth. And nowhere is this mission as clearly stated as in the story of a dinner party in chapter two of Mark's gospel (vv 15–17).

The story immediately follows the account of Jesus' call of Levi the tax collector, and tells of a shared meal that takes place (depending on how you translate the Greek) in Levi's house or in Jesus' own house. There were at table "many tax collectors and sinners…for there were many who followed him." Some scribes of the Pharisees were looking on, and they criticized Jesus for his disreputable choice of companions. Hearing their complaints, Jesus responded with this mission statement: "Those who are well have no need of a physician, but those who are sick; I have come to call not the righteous but sinners."

How striking and definitive these words are! Notice that Jesus doesn't say "I have come to call both the righteous and sinners," or "I've come to call everyone." No, he says that he has come to call some and not others—sinners, and not the righteous. His statement must have jolted those scribes who had censured him, as they lingered there at the edge of the feast. Jesus seems to be telling them that his mission focus doesn't include them—the most diligent practitioners of religious piety. At the same time, he makes it clear that he will not be pressured into more conventional religious behavior. His mission is to sinners and so with sinners he shall be. And therefore anyone who wants his company must be with sinners as well.

Thus Jesus offers an implicit challenge to his critics even as he rebuffs them. They don't have to stand off to the sidelines of God's work, judgmental and condescending. They can choose to give up their stance of superiority, and be with Jesus themselves. But theirs was a culture with clearly defined boundaries, and it would be no minor step for the scribes to cross that line into the society of sinners. They knew it would change the way others might see them; it would change how they saw themselves. It could even be interpreted by some as condoning sin, and thus could vitiate their role as models of purity in the community of faith. How were they to be differentiated from sinners if they associated with sinners? Still, how could they be associated with Jesus if they were determined to hold themselves aloof?

Seeing as Jesus did

"I have come to call not the righteous but sinners." The earthly Jesus first spoke these words to the scribes twenty centuries ago, and the risen Jesus speaks them now, in this age, to each of us personally and to all of us as the people of God. We too must face the challenge of this mission statement, even as the scribes of the Pharisees faced it. And we are confronted with the same difficult choice regarding how we see ourselves and how we see others and how we want others to see us. It is a choice that religious people have always resisted.

How do we see ourselves? Are we at least relatively righteous, comparatively virtuous, better than most? How do we see others? Are we quick to label their faults and transgressions, and so justify our frosty attitude toward them? Or do we perhaps rationalize our standoffishness with the mere suspicion that "he's not nearly so dedicated," or "she is hardly as good"? How do others see us? Do we cling to our polished reputation as "nice guy" or "generous-hearted" or "woman of faith"? Jesus' words re-echo to us: "...not the righteous but sinners." We had best be cautious, for the lines we draw could distance us from Christ.

Of course most of us would readily confess that we are sinners. Whatever our denominational background, as Christians we've been raised to understand that "all have sinned and fall short of the glory of God" as Paul so bluntly asserts in his epistle to the Romans (3:23). Accordingly, when we gather for communal worship we begin with an acknowledgment of our sin, and we seek God's forgiveness in our prayer and our song.

But even so, we may secretly pride ourselves on the fact that we are in church at all, that we pray, that we "know the Lord"—not like the many who live pagan lives devoid of spiritual commitment. And we all know the tendency to place ourselves at least a notch above those people we read about in the newspaper. No matter how dreadful our own offenses against God and others, we find comfort in observing how so-and-so has done even worse. "I'm not as bad as that one," we tell ourselves and whoever else will listen. And so we fall back into the mindset of the scribes in the gospel story, distinguishing ourselves from others based on comparisons of sin and righteousness.

Certainly there are degrees of iniquity, and some deeds are objectively more heinous than others. Yet who but God can judge whether our rationalized "little white lie" actually embodies less evil than another's flagrant sexual transgression? Who but God can judge if helping oneself to a few office supplies from work is really less grievous than another's store robbery? And who but God knows if our smug, condescending stance toward that petty office thief is not in the end more of an obstacle to holiness than the theft we condemn? It is, after all, itself a violation of Jesus' clearly stated commandment: "Do not judge…" (Matt 7:1). As John Henry Newman noted, "We are sinners, but we do not know how great. He alone knows who died for our sins."

It wasn't that long ago that in the United States we saw the rise of a Christian organization with an outrageous name: the Moral Majority. This epitomizes the religious temptation to exalt oneself morally over others, to name others as sinners and ourselves as righteous by comparison to them. How much this is like the Pharisee in one of Jesus' parables, who prayed "God, I thank you that I am not like other people: thieves, rogues, adulterers…" (Luke 18:11). That man went home, the parable tells us, unjustified—not right with God. Jesus' mission statement calls us to discard any such artificial distinctions between ourselves and anyone else. Such distinctions have no basis, and only serve to place us outside the mission focus of the Son of God.

Still, it keeps happening every day. A recent newspaper story told of a Catholic parish that held a special liturgy for gays and lesbians as part of an effort to reach people who were alienated from the church. The pastor explained how they wanted "to make sure that all people feel at home and loved in our churches," and to make clear that God loved everyone. Outside the church was a small band of protesters who greeted the attendees with placards reading "Shame!"

The reporter chatted with one of the protesters who described himself as a "faithful Catholic" and who proceeded to interpret the welcoming of gay persons as a condoning of sin. "Why don't they have a celebration of thievery next week?" the protester queried. It's the biblical story all over again: "I'm righteous and you're not." "I'm faithful and you're not." "I deserve to be welcomed at church, and you don't." And where is Jesus whenever this story is played out?

On the other hand, some Christians today, perhaps because of a past overemphasis on sin and guilt, have tried to seek spiritual balance and an improved self-image by denying the reality of sin entirely. If Paul sees that all have sinned and fallen short of God's dream for us, these believers insist that none have sinned, that no one is a sinner. While this approach succeeds in breaking down the barriers that religious people are prone to erect, it ignores what many writers have called the most empirically verifiable doctrine of Christian faith. It ignores Jesus' words—and indeed the teaching of the entire Bible—regarding our broken human condition. And it also reveals an erroneous understanding of what it means for us to see ourselves as sinners.

To identify ourselves as sinners is not the same as putting ourselves down or beating ourselves up. It is not the same as self-hatred; it need not cause us to dwell in a permanent state of guilt. As we enter into an experiential awareness of our sinfulness, it's true that at first we may feel disgusted with ourselves, confused, or filled with remorse. These are not pleasant feelings, but this does not mean they are bad for us. Just as another unpleasant feeling—fear—can keep us from a mugging in a dark side alley or prompt us to give up a health-damaging addiction, so the horror of our own sin can prompt us to give up relying on ourselves and to leap into the hands of God. There we discover with astonishment that God loves us despite our sinfulness, loves us with an infinite love and could not love us more if we were flawless! There we discover that we are totally accepted just as we are.

Sorrow gives way to joy. Guilt gives way to profound gratitude. And gratitude produces in us generosity of heart toward others. Because God loves us so unconditionally, we become more able to love ourselves and others that way as well. We no longer have any reason to deny our sinfulness, no reason to play "holier than thou." And this means we no longer have any need to scapegoat others, to project our dark side onto others, for we can freely own it ourselves—and still be at peace!

St. Ignatius realized this deep truth of the spiritual life through his own mystical experience, and incorporated it into his *Spiritual Exercises*. During the first week of the exercises, he leads the retreatant to confront the stark reality of sin before human history, within human history, and finally in the retreatant's own life. The typical and indeed sought-after response to this confrontation is revulsion, and those who are moving into the first week meditations are apt to describe their prayer experience as "difficult," "grueling," even "depressing."

Yet as the meditations of that week progress, the retreatant moves beyond despondency to a profound experience of mercy and grace. One woman told me, "I've never been so aware of my sin—and so joyful!" A clergyman told me, "It's funny that I have such serenity in the knowledge of my sin. I've spent my whole life running from this knowledge. Now that I've faced my guilt, I'm so much more open to God. I've become more likeable to myself and more compassionate to others." A college student said, "I don't want to forget my weakness and failure because I don't want to lose this awareness of how great God's love and power really are!"

If all then are sinners, and none are truly righteous, is anyone really excluded from Jesus' mission? It's clear that the only ones actually excluded are those who choose to exclude themselves. When we're wedded to our identity as morally superior, we can have little openness to the saving grace of God. When our pride is in how successfully we try to be good, and when we're quick to view the moral failures of others as being due to their lack of effort, what need is there of a redeemer? "Those who are well have no need of a physician," Jesus says. What can a doctor do if we won't acknowledge illness? Better the joyful cry of St. Paul: "Wretched man that I am! Who will rescue me from this body of death? Thanks be to God through Jesus Christ our Lord!" (Rom 7:24–25).

In his tender compassion, the living Jesus continues his mission to sinners, and those who have tasted their own sin continue to know his call. As Scripture testifies, where sin abounds, his grace abounds all the more (see Rom 5:20). The deeper and broader our life of sin, the more fervently the savior pursues us.

Hearing the call

Kevin knows the call of Christ. "The only commandment I didn't break was 'Thou shalt not kill'—at least, I don't remember breaking it," he says. Despite coming from what he describes as an idyllic "leave it to Beaver" upbringing, at nineteen years of age Kevin was a winner in beer-drinking contests and sleeping with any woman who'd let him. He partied through college, yet still landed a high-paying job with a national company. There he piled success on success, climbing upward in the corporation by brutally destroying any competition for higher positions. He says:

> All I cared about was money, sex, and power. I hung out in strip joints and treated women like objects—no different from my paycheck. At one time I was living with three different women at once, and none of them knew the others existed. And I had a wife at the time as well. Can you believe I actually walked out on my wife while she was in labor so I could be with my girls at the strip joint and drink? Marijuana and alcohol dulled whatever conscience I had left. It was a pretty dark period in my life, though I thought I was on top of the world.

Kevin nevertheless says he had a vague awareness of a presence that niggled him even as he sinned.

Over several years, his addictions to alcohol, sex, and money grew worse.

> Then it all collapsed. My wife divorced me, and my company was charged with securities violations. I lost the house and everything. When my wife told me she was leaving town with my kids, I went into heart fibrillation and landed in the emergency room. The doctors couldn't stop it, and told me I had a twenty-percent chance of surviving. I remember how scared I was. I cried out "If there's any power out there that runs the universe, could you please put me at one with it!" Incredibly, at once my heart went into normal rhythm. The doctors were astounded! My life had been saved, and when I got out I kept on the straight and narrow for a week and a half.
> Then I sank even lower. Still, I had a growing sense of some-

one with me, a power who wanted to help me. But I shut out that presence and plunged myself further in sex and alcohol. Only when I almost died a second time did I check myself into a rehab center. That was when I finally started to come to terms with the Presence. There was no overnight conversion, but a slow growth to knowledge. Like St. Paul, I asked "Who are you?" and like St. Paul, I came to know it was Christ. He's the one who had been with me all along. When I couldn't believe in him or in myself, he believed in me and kept after me. He saved my life. I could never express how grateful I am.

And so Kevin the drunken womanizer has become Kevin the devoted disciple of Jesus. Now he is ever alert to the ways in which he might reach out to others who are caught in destructive ways of life. He makes himself available whenever he can to encourage and support other men and women who are moving toward reform, or recovery from addictions. He's not afraid to speak of the reality of Christ and invite others to open themselves to Christ's power. "I know that no one's too far gone," Kevin says. "If he could reach me he can reach anyone. I want to help others receive what I've received."

This is Kevin's joy. Indeed, it is the great privilege of Christian life for all of us that we, the redeemed, are now able to share in the work of redemption. We are not merely the recipients of Christ's mission to sinners—we are invited to participate in that mission with him. We have been raised to the dignity of being his coworkers.

This honor should fill us with immense gratitude. Yet we must also recognize it as a sacred responsibility that is not optional for any of us. Jesus' priorities must be our priorities too—and he's made it clear that his focus is on "not the righteous but sinners." What does it mean for us as individual

Christians and as communities of faith to actualize that mission in our own lives? How do we make it real in our attitudes and behavior, our priorities in ministry, our expenditures of time and money?

Certainly we need to reflect on who are the religious and social outcasts of our own day. Who are the ones most likely to be labeled as "sinners" and shunned by the self-styled "righteous"? Standards have changed somewhat since biblical days. Agents of the Internal Revenue Service—the tax collectors of today—would probably not be on anyone's list of notorious sinners anymore. And many attitudes and acts proscribed in traditional Christian moral teaching are now widely accepted in secular society and even by some Christians. This of course does not mean these attitudes and acts are no longer sinful, but they no longer lead to ostracism as they once did.

What sort of sinner would you personally find morally reprehensible? Who would you be tempted to reject, ignore, shut out? What sort of sinner would not be well-received in your worshipping community were he or she to show up at your church door some Sunday morning? And what would it take for us as disciples to ally ourselves with Christ in his mission to that sinner?

The way in which we go about fulfilling that mission is of utmost importance, for as Christ embodied the compassion of the Father, so must we embody the compassion of Christ. In pursuing his mission to sinners, he who was sinless was never patronizing or sanctimonious. He sincerely loved and accepted people even when he didn't approve of their behavior. It was precisely this love and acceptance that more often than not moved the sinner to reform his or her life (see, for example, the story of Zacchaeus in Luke 19:1–10).

So in sharing Christ's mission to sinners, we who are sinners ourselves must never convey the impression that we're on some lofty spiritual plane, graciously condescending to minister to a far less worthy soul. Our words and our conduct must be rooted in the reality of our common human brokenness and our own ongoing need of the savior. In truth, as Paul writes, "There is no distinction..." (Rom 3:22). If we should find ourselves repulsed by the gravity of another's wrongdoing, we might find through prayer some of the love and mercy of Jesus, and make that known through our demeanor. Christ in us can melt the hardest of human hearts, just as he can melt our own often stony heart.

Some might fear that any association with grievous sinners opens us to bad influence, and possible temptation to greater sin ourselves. While we always need to be prudent in light of our own particular vulnerabilities, we don't need to be afraid. Jesus has overcome evil, and we can have faith that his power at work through us "is able to accomplish abundantly far more than all we can ask or imagine" (Eph 3:20).

As we know, the ancients were much concerned with what was clean and what was unclean. And it was believed that when the clean came in contact with the unclean, the clean was overcome and became unclean. (This was certainly a factor in the scribes' unwillingness to eat with sinners in the story examined above.) But Jesus demonstrated that the power of love and truth was greater than the power of evil and sin. So when love and truth come in contact with evil and sin, why worry that love and truth will be overcome? Rather, in the divine economy the unclean can become clean in Christ. This is what he accomplishes in each of us, and this is what he can accomplish through each of us for others.

Historians note that one of the reasons why the early church grew so rapidly was because of its welcoming attitude toward those whom ancient Judaism regarded as pariahs. Surely the first believers were motivated in this by the teaching and example of Jesus himself. More compelling still was their own experience of God's lavish forgiveness and love, an experience that by its very nature dissolves judgmentalism and inspires greatness of heart. "For the love of Christ urges us on," writes Paul, "From now on, therefore, we regard no one from a human point of view" (2 Cor 5:14, 16).

Today the love of Christ urges us on as well. We ourselves are graced beneficiaries of his mission to sinners; how can we not then make it our own? May no human prejudice or narrowness of vision keep us from seeing others as Jesus, the friend of sinners, sees them!

Questions for reflection

1. What examples of the "shun the sinner" mentality do you see in the church or society today? Can you think of any circumstances when this practice would be justifiable or even advisable? Read St. Paul's words in 1 Corinthians 5:9–13. How can his advice to the church in Corinth be reconciled with the teaching and practice of Jesus?

2. The chapter quotes John Henry Newman: "We are sinners, but we do not know how great. He alone knows who died for our sins." Do you agree with Newman's words? Do you think there will be surprises when the judgment day arrives?

3. Do you think that churches should hold special liturgies for people whose behavior is morally questionable, or even contrary to the morality espoused by the church? Why or why not? Do you think that welcoming someone to church is the same as condoning their behavior?

4. How do you think the church can preach the message of human sinfulness without leading people into self-hatred and despair? Can you relate to the experiences of the retreatants described in this chapter who were able to find joy in the knowledge of their sin?

5. These questions, which the chapter invites the reader to reflect on, would serve as a good basis for discussion as well. What does it mean for us as individual Christians and as communities of faith to actualize Christ's mission to sinners? How do we make it real in our attitudes and behavior, our priorities in ministry, our expenditures of time and money?

Four

A Mission to Serve

Parents hear it all the time—that seemingly endless squabbling among children for dominance. Who gets to go first? Who gets the best seat? Who's really the winner in that game's contested outcome? The bickering can almost become like cacophonous background music in the daily life of a family or neighborhood.

Children of course hear the same vying for dominance in the conversations of adults. Though it's usually more carefully disguised, it's woven into discussions of workplace intrigues, competition for promotions, who's "in" with the boss. Which relative makes more money? Which neighbor just spent more? Whose kid is most successful? Who has the pastor's ear? We can all get caught in this ongoing game that begins early in life and continues, for some, to the day they die. Like it or not, the craving for dominance often motivates our best effort. It funds preposterous salaries for professional athletes on "our team." It causes war.

Because this craving is so deeply rooted in our humanity, from the beginning people have tended to project it onto the divine realm as well. The gods in ancient mythologies were often depicted in bloody rivalries, fighting for supremacy or fending off human attempts at their thrones. They could be just as petty and power-hungry as any of their human devotees, and just as vindictive when they failed to get what they deemed to be proper homage.

Israel of old was not totally immune to this process of projection, and some of the things that are said of Yahweh early on in the biblical story seem more to reflect the religious immaturity of the people than the true nature of God. Yet over the centuries God's progressive self-revelation refined their understanding. Though omnipotent, God was not oppressive. God did not use the divine power to crush or demean; God was not coercive or punitive or cruel. Rather, the God they came to know was "merciful and gracious, slow to anger and abounding in steadfast love" (Ps 103:8). And further, as the teachings of the Law and the prophets made clear, God desired that these divine traits should be reflected in the behavior of the people. Thus the human desire for dominance over others was tempered with the principles of solidarity, mercy, and love.

Jesus was born into this rich tradition and was well versed in the teachings of his faith. Still, when the time came for him to begin his public ministry, the gospels tell us that he faced a time of grueling temptation. He knew he could pursue a path of domination and power that would fit the worldliest notions of messiah. After all, his people had long suffered under the yoke of foreign rulers, and he would no doubt win a following of thousands were he to issue a call to arms. Why not use power to subjugate those who had subjugated them? Why not flex divine muscle to quash injustice and make his voice heard? He could accomplish so much—even gain "all the kingdoms of the world and their splendor" (Matt 4:8). Why not dominate in the cause of God?

Yet he sensed in his depths that his call was to embody and reveal the God of Israel—the God he knew so intimately as his "Abba"—and he knew that God was not about domination. While many around him clamored for a military leader to overthrow the Romans and restore the Jewish nation as an earthly kingdom, Jesus was convinced that his messiahship must be of a different kind. He would not raise armies; he would not rout Israel's foes. To attempt it would be unfaithful, untrue to who he was, for God had sent him on a mission to serve.

Surely the Hebrew Scriptures played a key role in the formation of this mission awareness in him. Especially important, many scholars argue, were the four "suffering servant" poems found in the writings of a prophet now referred to as Second Isaiah (see Isa 42:1–9, 49:1–6, 50:4–9, 52:13—53:12). Chosen by Yahweh, formed by God in the womb, the servant is described as being sent on a mission of mercy, "to open the eyes that are blind, to bring out the prisoners from the dungeon, from the prison those who sit in darkness" (42:7). Gentle, yet strong in the face of adversity and suffering, the servant will bring salvation not only for Israel, but for all nations, and will remain faithful to God even when it results in suffering and death. Ultimately, that fidelity will lead to the servant's vindication.

As a plucked string causes harmonic strings to vibrate, so the words of these poems must have resonated in Jesus' heart as bespeaking his own identity and mission. And there's no question that they were prominent for the early church as well when they sought to understand and preach about Jesus' work among them, for in many places the New Testament writers draw on the language of these poems (see for example the passion account in Matthew's gospel, or the account of Philip's conversation with the Ethiopian eunuch in Acts 8:27–39).

Jesus sets forth his mission to serve explicitly in the tenth chapter of Mark's gospel (vv 35–45), at the conclusion of a story that must have been embarrassing for many in the early church. James and John, two men later known as great apostles and leaders in the faith community, appear in this story as rather thick-headed and self-seeking. (The rest of us who fall into this category might find some small comfort in their company!) As Mark tells it, the two approach Jesus to ask a favor they are reticent at first to name. "Teacher, we want you to do for us whatever we ask of you." Jesus replies, "What is it that you want me to do for you?" "Grant us to sit, one at your right hand and one at your left, in your glory."

Now before going any further in the story, we must note that Mark places this dialogue some time after Jesus' teaching on discipleship. ("If any want to become my followers, let them deny themselves and take up their cross and follow me...." 8:34ff.) And he places it immediately after Jesus' third prediction of his impending suffering and death in Jerusalem. So the reader of the gospel can't help but wonder: did these guys really not hear any of this? Did they just not get it? Did they really think they could outmaneuver the others and grab the best positions of honor? That hunger for dominance affects even such exemplary saints. No wonder the other men were angry! (The evangelist Matthew was apparently so embarrassed by this account that he tells it as the story of a good Jewish mother looking out for her boys—Matt 20:20–23. Luke just skips over it entirely.)

"Grant us to sit, one at your right hand and one at your left, in your glory." With incredible patience, Jesus responds to this request by insisting that true greatness is not found in the domination of others but in service to others. He asserts that leadership in his community is never to be authoritarian, repressive, or self-exalting. In this, the disciples must imitate Jesus' own example, "For the Son of Man came not to be served but to serve, and to give his life a ransom for many."

This saying is as emphatic in what it excludes as in what it includes, as was the case with the mission statement we considered in the previous chapter. Jesus' mission is to serve, not to be served. He did not come to "lord it over" people as the pagans do (Mark 10:42), though Lord indeed he is. He does not want the kind of submissiveness that a fearful inferior gives to a power-wielding superior. Unlike many of our human race, he doesn't get high on the adulation of others; he doesn't need them debased to feel strong himself. No, he wants to do the serving; he wants to lift others up.

Servant of all

John's gospel tells us that at the last supper Jesus enacted this mission symbolically in the washing of his disciple's feet (John 13:2–17). "Jesus, knowing that the Father had given all things into his hands, and that he had come from God and was going to God, got up from the table, took off his outer robe, and tied a towel around himself." He then proceeded to do that menial task normally assigned to a household servant, or performed by disciple for master and not the other way around. Peter protests such unseemly behavior, but Jesus will brook no objections. "Unless I wash you, you have no share with me," Jesus says.

Strong words, these! Peter needs once and for all to let go of his too worldly notion of how God's messiah should act—for

the mission of God's messiah is to serve! He had already been
rebuked at Caesarea Philippi for trying to keep Jesus from living this vocation (Mark 8:31–33). Now it was imperative for
him to accept this symbolic foot-washing in preparation for
accepting Jesus' ultimate act of service on the cross, when he
would "give his life as a ransom for many." Now, on the very
evening of Jesus' arrest, it was critical that Peter let Jesus live his
calling the way Jesus wanted to live it.

Perhaps we can sympathize with Peter, for we too look to
Christ as our master, and define ourselves as servants of the
Lord. Perhaps it is difficult for us to conceive of him serving us
today in so gracious and humble a fashion. Maybe all that was
just a temporary departure from behavior we'd deem more
appropriate for someone who is the Son of God. Maybe his
stint as servant ended on Calvary's hill.

No. God has not changed, and the living Jesus who perfect-
ly reveals God is, even in his glory, at this moment on a mission to serve.

Leona met this servant Christ, and her life was transformed.
She was in her mid-thirties, and new to a life of faith when she
attended a Christian conference on healing. On the first night
of the conference, the participants gathered for an outdoor
prayer service. Leona explains,

> I went, but I had my guard up from the beginning. Jesus for
> me at the time was very much a Jesus "out there" somewhere.
> I was very early on in the process of falling in love with him.
> It was a beautiful evening for the service—the temperature
> and the breeze and the sky were all perfect. At one point, the
> presenter invited us all to close our eyes, and led us in a guid-
> ed meditation. We were to visualize Jesus coming to us and
> asking to wash our feet.

I found myself drawn immediately and unexpectedly into an intensely real experience of the Lord. There he was, with towel and basin, asking me to sit down. Then he knelt before me, and all I could think was "This is the wrong position! He's not supposed to be below me, he has to be above!"

But he continued, and poured the water on my feet. It was so real I could feel it. And there was such tremendous care in his touch—so tender, so tender. I remember that I was afraid, and I kept telling myself not to look at his face, although I was very much moved to do so. Finally I looked. I looked down into his eyes, and he looked up into my eyes, and it spoke volumes about who I was and who he was. They were piercing eyes, but not uncomfortable. There are not enough words to say all that was in his eyes—they just melted me, and filled me with immense joy, a joy that has never left me, never!

I was oblivious to everything that happened after that. I couldn't get away from the eyes! And the positions! Without this experience of being served by Jesus I would never have known what service to others really was. I would probably have been just a churchperson!

Tears well up whenever she tells of this encounter. Leona is certainly far more that "just a churchperson" today, as she is on fire with love for her servant Lord, and spends her days in serving others.

In each of our lives, the living Christ comes not to be served but to serve, and, like Peter and Leona, we too may find it uncomfortable to see him so humbly bent over our feet. Peter was abashed by it; Leona was frightened. Yet accepting the service he offered was vital to their ongoing conversion process, and it's vital to ours as well. Who are we to say no to Jesus? Who are we to advise him?

In our day-to-day relationship with him, Jesus' goal remains the same. "I am among you as one who serves," he says to us (Luke 22:27). And unlike the other people who care about our well-being but who are, as we are, imperfect in love, Jesus' service is utterly without self-interest. There are no "hooks" in the help he gives; there are no hidden agendas. He's not keeping a running tally of what he does for us so that he can claim a payback down the road. He's not asking, "What's in this for me?" He's not scheming to see what he can get out of us. No, his concern for us is pure, and his activity in our lives is totally geared toward accomplishing our highest good. What an extraordinary friend to have!

And in Christ and through Christ the character of God is made finally plain, for "he is the image of the invisible God" (Col 1:15). In Christ and through Christ, so many of our common human projections and misconceptions about God are overthrown once and for all. Our Creator is revealed not as an overbearing potentate ruling from a distant throne, but as an attentive and caring companion. If Jesus' mission is to serve and not to be served, it is because that is the identity of God.

God's active love

This reality is expressed in a different way by the author of the first letter of John when he writes, "God is love" (4:8, 16). Often quoted, John's words are not saying that God is a fuzzy warm feeling somewhere in the sky; God is not an emotion. They tell us rather that our God is pure self-gift, that our God is eternally self-giving. Creation itself was an expression of love, for God had no need of a universe and no need of worshippers. God did not create for God's own sake, but for our sake! All creatures were made in an act of pure and simple goodness, that they might be the recipients of God's pure and simple goodness. As one theologian has phrased it, "Everything exists to be loved." And just as anyone who loves seeks to serve the beloved, so the One who is Love wants to serve us, and does serve us in all things. Service is love in action.

St. Ignatius, in his "Contemplation to Attain Love" at the conclusion of the *Spiritual Exercises*, offers a meditation to help the praying person grasp this mystery. He starts by reminding the reader: "Love ought to manifest itself more by deeds than by words" (1 John 3:18). He then invites us to remember all the gifts we have received from God, and to "ponder with deep affection how much God our Lord has done" for us. Many who pray through this exercise are astonished when they see how much God has been doing for them since the moment of their conception.

Further in the exercise he sets forth this point for reflection: "I will consider how God labors and works for me in all the creatures on the face of the earth; that is, he acts in the manner of one who is laboring." With these words, Ignatius goes beyond the obvious truth that God is everywhere. He wants us to perceive that this divine presence in all things is not static; God isn't just there. God is busy serving us! "He is working in the heavens, elements, plants, fruits, cattle, and all the rest," Ignatius writes. So, for example, God is actively working in the tree, causing it to exist at every instance, giving it life and color and every unique characteristic that makes this tree different from every other. And God is working in my body, enabling all the electro-chemical reactions that make it possible for me to see and touch and hear and enjoy the tree. And though billions of human souls now inhabit this earth, each of us is individually a recipient of God's active love, and each of us by grace might rightfully acclaim: this divine labor is given for me!

Indeed, God "labors and works for me," serving us continually, lovingly, and usually without our notice and without our thanks. It might be likened to the relationship between an infant and his or her parents. The parents are by far bigger, stronger, and smarter, yet they are dedicated night and day to the service of their child. The infant lives in an environment of care and protection, without any consciousness of the sacrifice and effort of the father and mother who maintain that environment. Nursed, diapered, bathed, dressed, carried, preened, and entertained, the little one receives it all simply as a matter of course. And that's just fine with mom and dad. They're not serving because they want praise or gratitude; they are motivated by the greatness of their love. No doubt the day will come when the child will see the truth of all that the parents have given, but for that little while there is no recognition of how totally dependent he or she is.

If human parents with their limitations and sin can serve so selflessly the child of their love, how much more must our God give in selfless labor on our behalf! God serves us freely and without concern for recompense, for God serves us in pure love. One day we shall fully see the enormity of all that God has done, though hopefully even now we are growing in our recognition of it, and finding our hearts overflowing with joy.

Here the prayer of the psalmist becomes our own: "What shall I return to the Lord for all his bounty to me?" (Ps 116:12). When we see that we are the beneficiaries of such lavish self-giving, we naturally want to give something in return. But can we be of any service to our servant Lord? When God made flesh tells us that he comes to serve and not to be served, will he even welcome our serving him?

Of course! While getting service from us is not his motive in coming, our desire to give it must bring him delight. We know from our human experience that true love is not conditioned on the beloved receiving it and loving in return—that's why there are so many pining and broken hearts in the world. But how gratifying it is when love is requited! In the same way, Jesus gives his loving service with no strings attached. But how pleased he is when we respond in kind!

Hence the Scriptures exhort us to render service to the Lord (see Luke 4:8, Rom 12:11). Hence the writers of the New Testament epistles often refer to themselves as servants of God or servants of Christ. Paul and James and Peter and Jude all begin their letters by identifying themselves with one of these titles, and are proud to be so identified. "Think of us in this way," Paul writes, "as servants of Christ and stewards of God's mysteries" (1 Cor 4:1).

Still, is it really possible for anyone to be of service to God, who is infinite and omnipotent? After all, as we read in the Acts of the Apostles: "The God who made the world and everything in it, he who is Lord of heaven and earth, does not live in shrines made by human hands, nor is he served by human hands, as though he needed anything, since he himself gives to all mortals life and breath and all things" (17:24–25). What do you give to the One who has everything? What does service to God in Christ mean?

When all things are considered, it appears that the only way we can give service to God is by giving service with God. In other words, the best possible response to Christ's mission of service in our lives is to join him in that mission by serving others. This is exactly what he tells us at the end of that foot-washing scene we considered before. Having astounded his disciples by under- taking the task, Jesus concludes it by saying, "If I, your Lord and

Teacher, have washed your feet, you also ought to wash one another's feet. For I have set you an example, that you also should do as I have done to you" (John 13:14–15). Receive my service, Jesus says, and pass it on! Let my mission to you become the pattern of your mission to others!

An old proverb states that imitation is the highest form of praise, and indeed we praise Christ when we imitate his loving service to others. The psalmist's query finds in this its answer. What shall I return to the Lord? Love and service to my fellow human beings!

Attentive to the needs of others

Perhaps nowhere is this message so evident as in the account of the last judgment in chapter twenty-five of Matthew's gospel. The Son of Man comes and is seated on his throne of glory. "All the nations will be gathered before him, and he will separate people one from another as a shepherd separates the sheep from the goats" (v 32). In his address to each group, the same litany of need is intoned: "I was hungry...I was thirsty...I was a stranger...I was naked...I was sick...I was in prison..." (vv 35–36, 42–43). And in each instance, the assembled are told that just as they did or did not serve "the least of these who are members of my family" they did or did not serve the Son of Man, Christ himself (v 40). It's a matter of simple, direct equivalency: service to others is service to God.

As Christians we may be so familiar with this text that we fail to hear its pointed, even shocking message. The scene suggests that the only valid measure of our devotion to God is whether or not we are of service to others. Strikingly absent are things that often place high on our list of what good Christians should be or do. There's no mention of the churchgoing habits of those

who are gathered; there's no mention of their doctrinal ortho-
doxy, or their life of prayer or lack thereof. These things are by
no means unimportant for the disciple of Jesus, but neither are
they primary. It all comes down to serving people; it all comes
down to the active imitation of Christ. "I have set you an example, that you also should do as I have done to you."

You and I are called to participate in the ongoing work of
Jesus by giving of ourselves in service. Following in the footsteps of the One who is our model, this requires of us careful
attentiveness to the real needs of others. Sometimes in our brokenness we can end up acting more out of our own need to
help than the other's need to be helped. Our service then
becomes self-serving rather than self-giving, an imposition,
just another form of domination.

Sometimes, unlike Christ, we may serve in order to create a
debt of gratitude we can collect on later, or in such a way that
we keep others in subjection to us, their own capabilities
thwarted and denied. This too is self-serving, manipulative, and
unworthy of Christ's name. It's true that none of us can attain
the purity of intention that we see in Jesus, but by grace we want
to grow in that direction. Prayer can help us keep our motives
in order, as can reading the Scriptures, and listening to the voice
of the Holy Spirit in the people and the world around us.

Sometimes fidelity in service may mean giving up comfortable pet projects that bear little fruit in favor of labors less to
our liking but more in tune with God's call. On such occasions,
our acts of self-sacrifice can unite us more closely with the suffering servant himself, who "did not regard equality with God
as something to be exploited, but emptied himself..." (Phil
2:7). There's no doubt about it—at times the service of others
can cost us dearly.

Once I was invited to give a retreat to an ecumenical group of clergy on the spirituality of ministry. I drew very heavily on this theme of Christ's service to us and our own call to serve others. During the break, one woman approached me and objected to the message, claiming that while it was important for white men to hear this, it did not apply to women or to oppressed minorities. "They've always been told to serve, and they don't need to hear it anymore," she told me. "They need to learn how to be assertive, and claim their rightful share of power."

I appreciate this pastor's concern, and I know that unscrupulous leaders have misused the language of service to continue their domination of others. But I don't see any exceptions for certain groups being made in Christ's teaching on this—especially as he was teaching to a group of disciples who were themselves members of an oppressed minority in the Roman empire, a group of disciples that included women.

In addition, I think her comments reveal a common misunderstanding of what service means. To give of ourselves in service does not mean letting others dominate us, nor does it mean confining ourselves to menial or manual labor. And of course we can be assertive and still serve others. There will always be people whom God calls to the exercise of authority ("power," if you will), and this call is given to them without regard to race or gender. As long as one exercises authority in a life-giving way, it can itself be a way of Christian service and a worthy goal for any believer.

According to John's gospel, after Jesus had washed the feet of his disciples, he spoke with them for some time in a most intimate manner. One might expect that, given his knowledge of the horror that awaited him the next day, this final discourse would be sobering if not depressing in tone. Yet these chapters

(14—17) are among the most sublime and uplifting in the entire New Testament. Many commentators have noted how, as Jesus' mission of service nears its culmination on Calvary, he seems to have already crossed into glory. He speaks of his joy, a joy he dearly wishes his disciples to share.

The key to sharing in that joy is sharing in that mission of loving service to others, even to the point of laying down our lives for them. How contrary this is to worldly understanding! We might more readily imagine the blissful life as a life of leisure, with eager subordinates waiting on our beck and call. But Jesus invites us to find our bliss not in being served but in serving. This is the way of the Most High and Almighty; this is the way for us all.

"If you know these things, you are blessed if you do them" (John 13:17).

Questions for reflection

1. What are some of the ways you see the human craving for dominance manifested in society? In your work, and social circles? In the church? Do you think it can ever bear good fruit for people? Why or why not?

2. Read the four suffering servant poems in the book of Isaiah (42:1–9, 49:1–6, 50:4–9, 52:13—53:12). Spend some time sharing what these texts mean to you. Given that we are all called to participate in Jesus' mission to serve, discuss how these poems might guide us in our Christian practice.

3. Leona had a powerful prayer experience that brought home to her the truth of Jesus' mission to serve. Have you experienced being served by Christ? How does Christ serve you today? How does it make you feel to know that the eternal Son of God wants to serve you?

4. "When all things are considered, it appears that the only way we can give service to God is by giving service with God." How might our service to others be affected if we saw it as collaboration with our servant God?

5. "As long as one exercises authority in a life-giving way, it can itself be a way of Christian service and a worthy goal for any believer." What's the difference between exercising authority in a "life-giving way," as opposed to a death-dealing way? How can we distinguish personally between an authentic call to serve in a position of authority, and an unspiritual craving for dominance?

Five

A Mission
to Give Life

Visitors to Mount Saviour Benedictine Monastery in Pine City, New York, cannot help but be touched by the beauty of that holy place on the hill. The clean air, the expansive sky, the sounds of birds and chapel bells, the simple yet sublime architecture of the monastery buildings, and the rhythm of prayer and chanted psalms—all make one's stay at Mount Saviour a memorable time of peace.

Perhaps most striking to those on pilgrimage from city or suburb is the panorama of fields and hillsides dotted with the white woolly shapes of hundreds of sheep. For the monks are shepherds, supporting their communal life by raising and selling sheep and lambs, wool and yarns.

It can be fascinating to observe the habits of the grazing flocks in the fields. They quickly scurry from a stranger who approaches the fence of the pasture, yet remain serenely undisturbed when one of the monks walks right into their midst— or rides in on a four-wheel dirt bike! The behavior of the sheep is almost comical on hot days when they push and squeeze one another, almost climbing on top of one another, to claim a modicum of shade in the small sumac grove near the road. This kind of up-close exposure to sheep and shepherding remains a bit of a novelty for most of us. But in many parts of the world, and for many cultures, it is an ordinary part of everyday life.

Certainly it was so for the ancient Israelites in biblical times. Their familiarity with the life of pastoral husbandry is reflected in the numerous references to sheep and lambs, flocks, shepherds, and sheepfolds that fill the pages of the Old and New Testaments alike. While most members of modern technological societies are at a disadvantage because of their lack of experience with these things, nevertheless the shepherding images we find throughout the Bible maintain a universal appeal. Is there a believer anywhere who has been unable to pray the words, "The Lord is my shepherd..." with meaning and fervor? (Ps 23:1).

Of course, Jesus made use of shepherding metaphors in his own teaching—the parable of the lost sheep and the description of the final judgment are two examples that might come immediately to mind (Luke 15:4–7, Matt 25:31–46). A third would be the well-known imagery of the sheep gate and the shepherd, found in chapter ten of John's gospel (10:1–18). Here, in a discourse much cherished by Christians, we find yet another of Jesus' mission statements.

Drawing on language from the rich biblical tradition in which he was formed, Jesus in this teaching speaks figuratively of his tender love for his flock, and his intimate knowledge of each member. "He calls his own sheep by name and leads them out...and the sheep follow him because they know his voice" (vv 3–4). In contrast to some of the religious leaders of his time whom he alludes to as "the stranger" and "the thief" and "the hired hand" (vv 1, 5, 8, 10, 12–14), Jesus describes himself as the good, or model, shepherd.

But his message stretches the bounds of the imagery because Jesus as good shepherd goes beyond what any earthly shepherd would reasonably be expected to do. If, on a typical farm, sheep might in due course forfeit their lives for the good of the shepherd (even the monks at Mount Saviour serve up some tasty lamb dishes!), here it is just the opposite. The good shepherd is so utterly dedicated to his flock that he lays down his life for them (vv 11,15).

Regardless of the cost, Jesus is determined to provide security and salvation for his own. This is his ultimate goal, his reason for coming. While "the thief comes only to steal and kill and destroy," Jesus says, "I came that they may have life, and have it abundantly" (v 10). He is absolutely clear about his mission, and he wants to make it absolutely clear to us as well.

Throughout the fourth gospel, the primacy of Jesus' mission to give life is reiterated in many ways. (The word "life" appears more times in John than in the first three gospels combined.) From the very beginning, we are told, the Word who is Christ existed as a source of life. "What has come into being in him was life, and the life was the light of all people" (John 1:3–4). Jesus elaborates on his mission in his conversations with Nicodemus, the woman at the well, and others (John 3:1–21, 4:1–26). He enacts it symbolically and dramatically in the raising of Lazarus from the tomb (John 11:1–44). And he brings it to its culmination when, crucified and risen, he breathes the Holy Spirit upon his disciples in the upper room. Through this Holy Spirit men and women are made children of God, and are filled with God's own life (see John 20:22, also 1:12–13, 3:5–8).

It is specifically God's own eternal life that Jesus came to give. He knew this eternal life within himself as the presence of his Father, indestructible and everlasting. "For just as the Father has life in himself, so he has granted the Son also to have life in himself" (John 5:26). And Jesus knew how passionately his Father desired to share this life with every soul on earth, with any who would receive it. That passion became Jesus' own, and motivated all that he did.

The mystery of shared life

It's not easy for us to grasp what it means to share God's life. Sure, we use similar language on occasion when talking about human relationships. We say, "They've decided to share a life together," or "I want to share my life with you." But when people "share life" with other people, they basically live their lives alongside each other. They may reside at the same place and do things together; they may talk about what they're feeling and reveal intimate details about who they are as persons. But they still remain separate individuals, outside one another. Their life experience remains uniquely theirs, never fully communicable. They may be for one another the closest of companions, even to their last breath, but however close they may be, ultimately they suffer and die on their own.

In Jesus, God is saying to us, "I want to share my life with you." But God isn't looking to just live alongside us as a close companion, or to be merely an important part of our lives— someone we might confide in from time to time, when we think to do it. God is looking to literally become one with us, to have us actually participate in the divine life of the Trinity! This is what we were made for. This is the meaning of salvation, and our most perfect fulfillment. And from before the foundation of the universe, this has been God's plan for us.

And once again, love is at the root of it. "For God so loved the world that he gave his only Son, so that everyone who believes in him may not perish but may have eternal life" (John 3:16). We know in our own experience that love, by its very nature, impels a lover to seek union with the beloved. We are the beloved of God, and how that infinite love burns with longing to become one with each of us in the unity of shared life! God's plan of salvation is in fact a centuries-long plan of seduction, as the divine lover wooed us and prepared us for oneness with the Trinity. In the coming of Jesus, that plan reached its consummation. Through Christ, with Christ, and in Christ, God tries to get inside us all.

"I came that they may have life, and have it abundantly," Jesus says. "This is indeed the will of my Father, that all who see the Son and believe in him may have eternal life" (John 6:40). Repeatedly in John's gospel, Christ's offer of life is put in the present tense—that is, it's an offer for the here and now, and not just a promise of what we'll receive after death. Here and now we can attain union with God by receiving divine life through faith in Christ and through baptism. Here and now, in our mortal state, we become charged with Christ's presence, which we bear with us in all our comings and goings, even in the most mundane of our daily activities. Our entire being is sanctified; we are made, as Paul writes, holy temples of God (see 1 Cor 3:16–17, 2 Cor 6:16). Were we to grasp the full import of this truth, we might well adopt the custom of bowing before one another, to acknowledge the indwelling God.

But like any image, Paul's image of the temple, though helpful, is insufficient for this mystery of shared life. God dwelt in the Jerusalem temple, but God never became one with the temple. In contrast, when we receive the life of God we do become one with God. And though we always remain creatures, by partaking in God's life we really "come to share in the divinity of Christ, who humbled himself to share in our humanity" (Roman liturgy). Our oneness of life with God is so profound that it can be said we truly become God. This is what Irenaeus emphasized in the second century, when he spoke of how Jesus "became what we are in order to make us what he is himself." St. Athanasius, two centuries later, said the same: "God became human that humans might become God." We are not walking tabernacles; we are, in a sense, God walking. Graced sharers in eternal life, whatever we do we do as one with God.

And whatever we do, we do as one with each other as well, for the life of God necessarily unites all of us who partake of it. This facet of the mystery is also beyond our comprehension, yet every bit as real. Paul struggled to convey it by speaking of the Christian community as the body of Christ, now organically bonded to each other in Jesus. "For as in one body we have many members, and not all the members have the same function, so we, who are many, are one body in Christ, and individually we are members one of another" (Rom 12:4–5).

Bringing about this unity among those who bear his name is not peripheral to Jesus' mission to give life. It was part of the divine scheme from the very beginning. Jesus earnestly desired it, and prayed that we might all be one, that we might experience the joy of loving union with each other even as Jesus himself found joy in his loving union with the Father. "As you, Father, are in me and I am in you, may they also be in us... I in them and you in me, that they may become completely one" (John 17:21, 23). Our mystical communion in God's life will also become visible in how we treat each other, especially the least among us. According to the gospel, this loving unity is the best testimony we can give to the Presence and truth of Christ in an unbelieving world (see John 13:35, 17:21, 23).

Clearly, then, the abundant life Jesus came to give is not something ethereal and of little significance for our earthly existence. It is not what the cynic calls "pie in the sky, by and by." Though God's life present in us is different from the natural, mortal life we received through our parents (see John 3:6), it increasingly enhances every dimension of our natural life in very real and even concrete ways. It permeates and transforms our thinking, feelings, and intuition, leading inevitably to changes in our behavior—indeed, in our whole way of being in the world. We begin to see things differently as we begin to see them in God. We become more sensitive to human suffering in its many forms—suffering that earlier we may never have noticed—and more motivated to do something about it. We are able to be more truly present to the people we live with, more attuned to their joys and sorrows, and more compassionate in our dealings with them. Jesus' mission encompasses all of this and more. His intent is that, filled with divine life, we should live every aspect of life with greater intensity and relish.

Physical effects

As we surrender ever-deeper levels of ourselves to God's desire for union, the divine life may be manifested even in our bodies. We are, after all, incarnate beings, and our physical nature is inseparable from our spiritual identity, or soul. Hence, religious people throughout the ages have reported heightened acuity of the five bodily senses as one common accompaniment of spiritual experience and growth in Christ. (See my earlier book *Spiritual Surrender: Yielding Yourself to a Loving God,* chapter four, "Surrender in Pleasure and in Joy.") Sensations felt in the body itself are also common, especially during times of prayer—everything from vague feelings of warmth or tingling, through such dramatic mystical phenomena as stigmata, levitation, bi-location, and ecstasy.

Contemporary neurological research has pinpointed some of the electro-chemical occurrences in the brain that constitute the physical component of religious experience. This research in no way undermines the authenticity of that experience, but helps us to appreciate how spirit and flesh intersect in us. "I praise you, for I am fearfully and wonderfully made" (Ps 139:14).

John of the Cross, the great mystic and doctor of the church, had quite a bit to say about the possible physical effects of God's life in us. He tells us that, as our union with God intensifies,

> sometimes the unction of the Holy Spirit overflows into the body and all the sensory substance, all the members and bones and marrow rejoice, not in so slight a fashion as is customary, but with the feeling of great delight and glory, even in the outermost joints of the hands and feet. The body experiences so much glory in that of the soul that in its own way it magnifies God.

Just as on occasion we might taste God's life within our own being, God's life in other people can also become evident to our senses. This is why traditional iconography depicts Jesus and the saints with glowing halos, attempting to convey how even in their outward form, the radiance of God's life was somehow apparent. And if you've ever known a truly holy person, you know how perceptible the life of God in them can be.

I think immediately of a man I knew for nearly twenty years. He was sixty at the time I met him, and newly retired from a career at a major pharmaceutical company. When our paths first crossed, Joe told me how he had recently and unexpectedly come to a profound new awareness of God's love for him. Though he had always been a man of strong faith, he said he felt like he was becoming a Christian for the first time. He'd tell anyone who would listen: "I lived all these years, and never knew how much God loved me! I'm so grateful! I've never been so happy in my whole life!"

While others in his situation—he was single and financially secure—might fill their retirement with leisure pursuits, Joe gave himself wholeheartedly to volunteer work and learning more about his faith. He took courses in Scripture, led Bible study groups, and taught Christian meditation. And whenever he spoke of Jesus, his face would noticeably light up. He'd break into a beaming smile, and sometimes his eyes would even fill with tears. "I'm so happy," he'd say "I never would have believed you could be this happy." The life of God shone visibly in him, and I wasn't alone in recognizing it. All who met him would comment on it, and simply being around him could lift the spirits of the most cheerless souls.

In his late seventies, his health deteriorated, and he was diagnosed with a rapidly progressing neurological disease that within a year landed him in a nursing home. There, paralyzed and bedridden and breathing through a respirator, his body curling into a fetal position, Joe remained radiant. When he was able to speak, he never complained to visitors, but would say things like "That tree outside my window is so beautiful in the sunlight. God keeps blessing me and blessing me." The nurses at the home told of how he brightened their day. The respiratory therapist said he told everyone about Joe. "As Christians we're always talking about the beatitudes," the therapist said to me one day as he adjusted Joe's ventilator tube, "but this guy really lives them! I always look forward to seeing him—he's been such a gift to me." Even as Joe's body withered away, the abundant life of Christ shone through him, palpable and real. He died the death of a saint.

The divine life can become just as palpable in us—and more so—if we let Jesus have his way. In this we must be patient because growth in God's life is a gradual process, a journey, a deepening love affair. We can hinder its pace by our sin, which is why we need to stay alert to the occasions when our unregenerate "old self" might get in the way (see Rom 6:6, Eph 4:22, Col 3:9). But we cannot rush our growth as if it were simply a matter of putting in spiritual effort. For no matter what we do and no matter how hard we may work, we can't earn eternal life for ourselves. It always comes as sheer grace. It is always the work of Christ.

Paths to abundant life

At the same time, we are not merely passive recipients of what Jesus brings. We are not like inert bottles into which he pours God's life, nor is growth in that life something that "happens" to us automatically, like growing older with the passing of years. Like Mary's "yes" at the annunciation, our cooperation is essential if Christ is to further his mission in us—for we do have a choice in this matter of our salvation. Continually he offers his gift, holding it forth to us on nail-scarred hands, eager for us to accept it. Continually, he urges us to "take hold of the eternal life" (1 Tim 6:12) through the active practice of our faith, and to "choose life," in every time and circumstance (Deut 30:19).

Prayer is one way we take hold of the gift Jesus offers. Regardless of how we do it, or what words we use, or if we use any words at all, the simple act of becoming consciously present to God in prayer allows God to possess us more completely, and fill us with life. Whether it happens in sustained periods of devotion or in fleeting moments during the course of a day, whenever we choose to pray we are choosing life.

With prayer, quality—not quantity—is primary. In our human experience, we know how a short but intimate time with a friend is more invigorating and nourishing to our relationship than two hours of guarded small talk. It is the same in our relationship with God. Honesty, sincerity, and above all a willingness to let God get close, even when we find that a bit frightening, can turn ten minutes into a life-giving encounter with the Creator. In contrast, if we hold ourselves in reserve and God at arm's length, two hours of religious activity will prove much less fruitful, and more frustrating to ourselves and to the giver of life as well.

We can also open ourselves to an influx of the abundant life by reading the Bible, and studying it, and reflecting on it. Christian people have always treasured the words of this book as a privileged meeting place with Christ, who is the word of God incarnate.

The importance of God's word as a source of life could hardly be overemphasized, so often is it affirmed in the Scriptures and in the Christian tradition. Jesus himself calls upon us to make his word our home, promising that it will set us free, and preserve us from death (John 8:31-32, 51). In his conversation with the tempter, he cites a passage from the Old Testament: "One does not live by bread alone, but by every word that comes from the mouth of God" (Matt 4:4). The first part of this saying is often quoted, and sometimes outlandishly misused to justify all kinds of things. But we need to focus on the second part—on the truth that we mortal creatures live by every word that comes from the mouth of God. If we want to take hold of eternal life, we'll want to take hold of the Scriptures, frequently and devotedly. "Indeed, the word of God is living and active," writes the author of Hebrews (Heb 4:12). And what believer has not found it so? What believer has not been revitalized through contact with God's word?

In the sacrament of the Eucharist we are given yet another opportunity to take hold of the eternal life Jesus gives to us. In the sixth chapter of John's gospel, where Jesus identifies himself as "the living bread that came down from heaven," (v 51) we hear him say: "Those who eat my flesh and drink my blood have eternal life, and I will raise them up on the last day; for my flesh is true food and my blood is true drink. Those who eat my flesh and drink my blood abide in me, and I in them. Just as the living Father sent me, and I live because of the Father, so whoever eats me will live because of me" (vv 54–57).

In the concreteness of the Eucharist, in our eating of bread made his body and wine made his blood, we can experience so many elements of Christ's mission to give life. This is why its celebration is so widely regarded by believers as the pinnacle of Christian worship.

In the Eucharist we experience Jesus' total self-giving as the good shepherd, who not only laid down his life for his flock, but also gives himself for our food. We physically take him into ourselves, where his body and blood are absorbed into our own and we are absorbed into him. In the flesh, here and now, we become one with him in the divine life he shares with his Father and he becomes one with us in this life that we live in the world. In the flesh, here and now, we actualize our communion with each other as well. We can see it happening at liturgy as body after body consumes his body, and like a divine catalyst he forges us into one. "Because there is one bread, we who are many are one body, for we all partake of the one bread" (1 Cor 10:17).

In addition to the practice of prayer, Scripture reading, and Eucharist, we can also embrace abundant life—or not—in the routine decisions we face every day, many of which affect not only our own future but the future of other people as well. What career do I choose? Shall we have another child? Shall I resign from this job? Do we move mother into a nursing home or care for her here? There's not always a right and a wrong answer to questions like these. But in every situation, the better course of action will be the one that leads to greater life, for this is God's will for us, made plain in Christ Jesus.

The need for discernment

The path that leads to greater life, however, may not always be readily apparent, or the one to which other people might steer us. For this reason we need to reflect on our choices in prayer, asking Christ to guide our discernment, and staying attentive to what's going on in our own heart and mind. The path to greater life may not always prove to be the easiest path either. Sometimes we may endure many little deaths in walking it. (Remember that Jesus was choosing life for himself and all of us as he trudged his way to Calvary, a heavy cross upon his shoulders.) And because each of us is unique, I may find more abundant life along a different avenue than the one you've been called to travel.

Talking with a spiritual director about decisions we are facing can be most helpful in discerning the way to greater life. I'll always remember how my own director, a Jesuit, ministered to me at a time when I was struggling with a choice. He asked me to talk at length about both options, first one and then the other. And then he simply reported back to me what he had seen as I talked. He said:

> I noticed that when you talked about the first option, your eyebrows knit together, and your eyes narrowed, and the muscles around your mouth got tighter, and your body seemed to tense up. Then, when you talked about the other one, I witnessed just the opposite. Your eyes widened, and even seemed to twinkle. There was a bit of a smile as you spoke, and you sat up taller—your whole demeanor was more animated. I get the impression that there's more life associated with that choice than with the first one. Does that resonate with you?

His observation hit me with the force of truth, and I was at once clear about what I needed to do. The path I chose was the more difficult of the two, but there's no question that it was the path of more abundant life in Christ.

Engaging faithfully with Jesus day by day, in these ways and others, enables him not only to fulfill his mission in us, but also to further it through us. For while we cannot give out God's life to those we meet, the vibrancy of that life in us will certainly prove attractive to many and draw people to Christ. What a joy it is when our witness, as individuals or as communities of disciples, helps bring another soul to abundant life! Then we realize our vocation to be a light to the world, and a city built on a hill (see Matt 5:14–16).

But we can also hinder Jesus' ongoing mission to give life. This happens when we don't stay open to Christ ourselves, and it results inevitably in a lack of vitality that no one would find attractive. In fact, sometimes Christians have given the impression that believing in Christ brings less abundant life. Too often, people have looked at us and seen, not a spiritual vibrancy but a dour religiosity that has no connection at all to the joyful news Jesus preached. Too often they've heard us talk about our faith with emphasis on "don't do," "can't have," "not allowed to," rather than on what we can do as the people of God, what we have as sharers in divine life, what privileges are ours as Christian people.

In addition, under the guise of godliness, we have sometimes hidden from the risks and challenges of engagement with secular society, letting our fears or personal hang-ups keep us from living fully in this world. Sometimes it seems we have even lost sight of the gospel entirely, bickering among ourselves over minutiae of doctrine or church practice. In Flannery O'Connor's novel *Wise Blood*, the character Hazel Motes tells a woman on the train, "If you've been redeemed, I wouldn't want to be." How many people might look at us and say the same thing?

One young man, Jason, was amazed to discover the negative impression some people have of Christian faith. He tells of how shortly after his conversion to Christ, he attended a family reunion where he saw many relatives he hadn't seen for years. Jason says,

> Word had already gotten around that I had "found religion." Several of my aunts and uncles said things like, "You're too young to be a religious. Save that until after you've had a little fun!" One of my cousins, who'd obviously been drinking too much, spent quite a bit of time trying to convince me that I should "give up all this Christian stuff and really enjoy life." When he could see that he wasn't convincing me, he sighed and staggered off in another direction. All I could think as I watched him was: How we have missed the boat as a church!

So many people actually think that believers don't enjoy life and don't have fun—why, I've never enjoyed life so much as I have since I've met Christ!

After this experience, Jason was determined to avoid contributing to such unfavorable perceptions of Christianity. He says, "I know none of us is perfect, but as believers we have a responsibility to represent Christ accurately. The only way people can know what abundant life means is by seeing us living it." Jason's comment is worth remembering—a good challenge for us all.

For all its richness and beauty, the eternal life that pulses and grows within us remains but a foretaste of the union we shall one day enjoy. Given by Christ and lovingly tended by him, it is carrying us to an unimaginable glory. For when our natural lives fade into the darkness of death, the persons who we are will keep on living with the indestructible life of God. "Those who believe in me, even though they die, will live," Jesus promised (John 11:25). No longer bound by space and time, no longer fettered by our sin and creaturely limitations, we shall know such an intensity of life in God that this life, even in its most exalted moments, will seem but a pale shadow in comparison.

Then, the good shepherd's dream of abundant life for his flock will attain its fullest realization. Then, and only then, will his mission have reached its end.

Questions for reflection

1. Read John 10:1–18. What lines particularly touch you? What do these verses say to you about our relationship with Jesus? Do you find the shepherding imagery helpful, or not? Can you think of other ways to convey the same message without using shepherding imagery?

2. Christians sometimes speak of eternal life as something we receive when we die. Have you thought this way also? How might it change the way we look at ourselves or others, if we realize that we share God's life right now, and that we are so loved by God that God wants to become one with us?

3. As Jesus so earnestly desired that we should be one in him, what might we do to foster greater unity among Christians and among churches?

4. Can you relate any stories about how God's life in you has changed the way you see things, or made you more compassionate and attuned to the needs of others? Have you ever experienced physical manifestations of God's life, for example, sensations felt in the body, or heightened acuity of the senses? Can you relate any stories about someone you have known in whom God's life was somehow apparent?

5. The chapter focuses on four spiritual disciplines as ways of opening to God's life: prayer, reading Scripture, Eucharist, and discernment. How have you experienced God's life coming to you through these practices?

Six

A Mission
to Bring Fire

The sky may still be blue when its first distant rumblings touch the edge of our consciousness—was that thunder? Within minutes the suspicion is confirmed as again, and then again, it ripples the air, each time a little louder. Then the wind darts out of the trees, here and there, in gusts and eddies, scattering leaves and papers and the calm of a quiet day. The warning has been given: a storm is on its way.

Sometimes you can watch it move in, heavy and solid like a dark curtain being drawn across the firmament. Sometimes it seems more furtive, starting out as wispy strands of vapor that slowly yield to thicker, more ominous clouds. Sometimes you can even smell it coming, as those who live close to nature will attest—there's a certain sharpness in the air that only the nose knows.

The prudent will find shelter before the storm is overhead, before the driving rains or hail come beating on the earth. We've not much time to linger out of doors, though the churning gray atmosphere can hypnotize and hold our gaze. The first few drops hasten our flight, as the wind, now more constant, rises.

And then it hits. Water is pouring down, streaming and pooling in streets and driveways, as trees are stretched by the force of the gale. But it's the lightning that takes our breath away—the sudden flash, the searing streak, the startling crack that shakes the house, followed by another and another. Something awesome is in progress; we may feel exhilarated, and a bit afraid. Despite all our scientific explanations, a thunderstorm can still humble us with its might.

In primitive ages, such celestial events must have terrified our earliest ancestors. Yet if, on the one hand, they would have dreaded the storm and hidden from its fury, on the other hand, they surely would have welcomed the gifts a storm could bring—for those dark clouds provided much needed rain, and those lightning strikes brought fire from above. Of the two, no doubt water was treasured as more immediately essential for life—especially in warmer, more arid climates where dry lands and dry throats were known to bring diminishment and death. But it was fire that eventually made civilization possible. Fire could light and heat the night, protect from wild animals, and make more foods fit for consumption. It could transform clay into vessels and cooking pots, and form metals into tools and weapons.

And it was fire, so insubstantial and mysterious, that our ancestors viewed as closely connected with the divine. In some cultures, fire was itself worshiped as a god. In others, its divine origin was expressed through images of deities with thunderbolts or through elaborate myths of how fire came from heaven to earth.

In the Bible, lightning and fire appear often as manifestations of God's presence. It's in a burning bush that Moses encounters God, and in fire and lightning at Mount Sinai

(Exod 3:1–6, 19:16–18). In a pillar of fire, God stayed with the Israelites through their desert wanderings, and in a cloud of fire hovered over their desert tabernacle (Ex 13:21, Num 9:16). Indeed, Moses tells the people, "The Lord your God is a devouring fire" (Deut 4:24; see also Heb 12:29). Lightning and fire also feature prominently in the visions of prophets like Ezekiel and the New Testament seer John (see for example Ezek 1:13, Rev 1:14, 4:5). And sometimes, fire represents God's judgment and wrath, as in the Genesis story of Sodom and Gomorrah, or the burning lake in the book of Revelation (Gen 19:24, Rev 20:10, 14–15).

Fire is such a potent symbol in Scripture—or in any literary or artistic work—because our human experience with fire has been so longstanding and multifaceted. Even today, fire's tremendous power can rouse fear in us. Its potential for destruction is immense, for a tiny spark can become an inferno that levels city and forest. And flames once ignited cannot always be controlled. Yet we know fire too as a source of security. We do not want our house on fire, but we want a fire to warm us inside our house. We curl up before it on a winter's eve and find comfort in its presence. Each day when the sky is blue we can look up to watch a ball of fire creep from east to west. We are conscious that it's fire that makes life on this planet possible and pleasant. Hence, the image of fire can touch us on a very deep level. It can unsettle us whenever we come upon it, and stir up many different feelings and associations, both positive and negative.

This is why Jesus so readily captures our attention in the Gospel of Luke when he uses the image of fire to describe his mission on earth. And though his words were uttered many centuries ago, we still can sense the passion and intensity that lay behind them, for in these words, he tells of a burning desire in his heart. "I came to bring fire to the earth," Jesus exclaims, "and how I wish it were already kindled!" (Luke 12:49).

What a startling image of the Savior—Jesus as a fire starter, Jesus as a benevolent arsonist! We may be more comfortable picturing him with a lamb on his shoulders or a jeweled book tucked under his arm, than with a torch in his hand, eager to set things ablaze! Yet, he tells us, that's precisely what he wants to do. And people being too comfortable may be just why he wants to do it.

Several centuries before the birth of Christ, the prophet Malachi told of the approach of a purifying messenger of God. "Who can endure the day of his coming," Malachi wrote, "and who can stand when he appears? For he is like a refiner's fire..." (Mal 3:2). In his own time, Jesus was like a refiner's fire. Standing on the firm foundation of the Jewish faith that he so treasured, he became a compelling force for religious renewal.

To be sure, his words and deeds could be inflammatory, destabilizing people's assumptions about God and turning the contentions of his opponents to ash. He openly challenged Sabbath regulations that coerced and constrained when they were meant to set souls free. And he contested purity rules that isolated those most in need of God's love. Some hypocritical members of the religious elite, in particular, felt his blistering critique (Matt 23:13-39), as did those who refused to believe that God was at work through him. And his prophetic outburst against corruption in the temple was guaranteed to win him enemies. But Jesus' fiery zeal would not be quenched, for he could see the gold amidst the dross. He knew what Israel had been given, and saw what Israel could yet become.

He was like a refiner's fire for the individuals who knew him too, keenly aware of what each could become. Relationship with him always seemed to involve something going up in smoke, so that a truer self might break through. At first it was just boats and nets that the fishermen had to give up. But later it was their petty rivalries, their envy, and their fears, for they were being forged into disciples. Seven demons blocked Mary of Magdala and had to be cast out. Zacchaeus had to lose his greed, Nicodemus his narrowness of vision. Jesus led sinner after sinner to the furnace of repentance, and brought them out made new.

Of course, Paul knew well the purifying fire of Christ. When, on that road to Damascus, he was plunged into "light from heaven, brighter than the sun" (Acts 26:13), his former life was virtually incinerated. Yet he had been so sure about who was right and who was wrong in that conflict with the Christians! And he had felt so secure behind the walls of his theological certainties! But now the whole edifice had been burned down with a suddenness that was staggering. From the aftermath of pain and confusion, Paul emerged as the man he was called to be. (The seeds of some plants can only germinate after exposure to charring flames. St. Paul, it seems, was like those seeds.)

Conversion and desire

The living Jesus brings purifying fire to each of us as well, a fire that can burn up, and burn down, much of what we cling to. As we let him draw close, we may even feel like parts of who we are are being scorched away. The saints tell us that every level of our being will eventually be affected—memory, intellect, emotions, will, imagination, and sense—as little by little, or in fits and starts, Christ's work of purgation proceeds.

It's not uncommon, especially when we're newly converted,

to begin wondering who we really are, as we see what little substance there is to the person we've always been. We may find that we can't go on wearing the mask we once wore, doing the work we once did, playing the games we once played. We may be surprised to discover that our tastes have drastically changed and that what we once coveted now has no appeal. For the old self has died (Rom 6:6, Eph 4:22–24), and is being cremated.

No one claims this process will be pleasant, and the spiritual hedonist may choose to walk away. But even in the midst of it we can sense that something wonderful is afoot. We can glimpse the beauty of who we are in Christ already beginning to shine, and the glorious life we'll one day have when the refining fire is done.

Thomas Merton, the twentieth-century Trappist monk and spiritual writer, told of his own journey to conversion. It was a journey that led him from a wild and licentious youth to the doors of Gethsemani Abbey in Kentucky, a journey that he understood would continue in the monastery until the day he died. At the end of his autobiography, *The Seven Storey Mountain*, he writes of a prayer experience in which he heard the voice of God. "Everything that touches you shall burn you, and you will draw your hand away in pain, until you have withdrawn yourself from all things," he heard God say. "Everything that can be desired will sear you, and brand you with a cautery, and you will fly from it in pain, to be alone."

Yet Merton's purification, like Paul's, would lead to great things: "And your solitude will bear immense fruit in the souls of men you will never see on earth," God continued, "...and I shall lead you into the high places of my joy and you shall die in Me and find all things in My mercy which has created you for this end." While Merton's path in life was unique, as is true for all of us, many have found in the words he heard a description of their own journey with God.

If at times we know fire as purifying, we also know fire in a different guise—the fire that smolders in a lover's heart, the heat of passion, the fever of desire. In every age, in every land, in lovers' words we hear of fire, for nothing else captures the experience so vividly and so well. "Love is strong as death," wrote the author of the Song of Songs, "passion fierce as the grave. Its flashes are flashes of fire, a raging flame" (8:6). And the same imagery appears over and over in countless poems down through the centuries.

Ever faithful to his mission, Jesus brings fire that enflames us with love and fills us with desire for God. We see it in the days of his earthly walk, when his appearance on the scene of first-century Palestine aroused a holy fervor in the populace. Large numbers followed him, and mobbed him when he appeared in their towns, or in the nearby countryside. They came because they wanted to. They wanted what Jesus was offering; they wanted God. Many may never have known what they longed for until they had contact with him. But he gave direction and strength to their longing, and so brought them to the arms of God.

In story after story, we see how Jesus inspired people to praise the God of Israel, and to trust in God's love anew. Such warmth of affection he kindled in that woman who wept on his feet, then kissed and anointed them with oil (Luke 7:36–50). Mary of Bethany was so enthralled by his words she could only sit at his feet in wonder (Luke 10:38–42). And the possessed man, set free, who begged to stay with him, was filled with that fire as well (Mark 5:18).

What was it that brought the crowds to this prophet from

Nazareth? What sparked so much godly devotion in so many of his contemporaries? Was it the content of his message? Was it the healing power that went out from him? Without question, both of these drew the attention of the multitudes, and had a profound influence on people's spiritual lives.

But often, as we know, it's not just what gets said and what gets done that's important—how it is said and how it is done can make all the difference in the world. (Think of an insightful sermon read in a monotone voice by a disinterested preacher. Think of food being brought to a poor family by a judgmental and resentful volunteer.) The gospels make clear that how Jesus said and did things made what he said and did so effective. He spoke with authority and conviction. He looked at people with tenderness. He prayed with great intensity. He touched with great compassion. In short, Jesus himself was on fire with love for God his Father, and with love for those he met. This is what others found so attractive in him; this is what so moved them within. And thus the fire was spread by contagion.

Growing in love

The risen Jesus still burns with that great love today, still cares deeply, still touches with compassion. If we truly give him our attention in prayer—that is, move our eyes away from the various troubles that beset us, and suspend our constant navel-gazing—we can see in him the blazing passion that the crowds saw long ago. In Christ, here and now, we are made privy to that uncreated energy of love that is God's very nature, the love that binds the Father and the Son in an eternal dance of joy, the love who is God the Holy Spirit.

At times we can feel overwhelmed simply being in the presence of the divine ardor. If we thought we knew what love was all about, this experience quickly dispels the illusion—for we find we are like a half-lit coal in attendance at a conflagration. Yet Jesus invites us to come closer and not back away, as he gently fuels and fans the flames of love in us.

And as love grows, our desire grows as well—for don't these two go hand-in-hand? We are filled with a longing for God that is itself a tremendous gift from God. This longing keeps us focused on God and motivates our spiritual practice. If earlier our energies were pulled in diverse directions by unhealthy worldly attachments, desire for God reorients them and gives us singleness of purpose, greater purity of heart. When we fall in love, desire for the beloved becomes all-consuming.

Yet while our longing for God is a blessing, it can be a source of restlessness and a persistent ache. When the stomach is empty, we prowl through cupboards and drawers, or leave our desk in search of food. When sexual desires awaken within, they preoccupy and distract our minds, yearning to be fulfilled. In similar fashion, spiritual desire can disquiet us.

But unlike the various hungers of the flesh, which can find momentary satisfaction, our desire for God actually increases in God's presence. The more of God we experience, the more of God we want. We eat blissfully at the sumptuous banquet that Christ spreads before us, and we become hungrier for God with each bite, ever more desirous of total union. As John of the Cross writes, even in advanced stages of holiness, the soul "still lives in hope, in which one cannot fail to feel emptiness....However intimate may be a man's union with God, he will never have satisfaction and rest until God's glory appears."

It's not uncommon for men and women who seek spiritual direction to tell of restlessness and desire as the reason for their coming. Because we are so conditioned, especially in the developed countries, to expect that all our wants can be promptly satisfied, some may be surprised to hear that there's no panacea for this spiritual longing. What is called for is a change in attitude. We need to recognize that our rising desire is the work of Jesus in us, and a sign of growth in love. It serves God's good purpose, and it will not go away—at least not in this life. So it's best for us to embrace the longing, feel it, sit with it, and express it in our prayer. Then we will find, paradoxically, that this holy desire is itself far more fulfilling than any of the world's delights. Then we will find, paradoxically, that in wanting God we know God.

When someone's in love, we may notice that they have a certain glow about them, a glint in their eyes and a readiness to smile—often for no apparent reason. And they seem excited simply to be alive. They seem confident about the future, because they believe that with their beloved at their side they can face anything.

Many of these same signs mark those men and women in whom Jesus has lit the fire of divine love. They begin to live with joy and confidence, and they exhibit a great hope that can sustain them through every difficulty. St. Paul expresses it well when he writes,

> Who will separate us from the love of Christ? Will hardship, or distress, or persecution, or famine, or nakedness, or peril, or sword? ...No, in all these things we are more than conquerors through him who loved us. (Rom 8:35, 37)

No doubt we've felt that joy and confidence ourselves and have been sustained by that enduring hope. No doubt we've displayed those smiles that come unbidden and that excitement to be alive. Indeed, to one degree or another, we know what it's like to be on fire with love for God, and on fire for

Christ Jesus. Like the prophet Jeremiah, we may have felt that fire burning in our bones, stirring us to speak and act, prompting us on to where we might not otherwise have gone (Jer 20:9). Like those men on the road to Emmaus, we may have felt that fire burning in our hearts as we awakened to the presence of the Risen One at our side (Luke 24:13–35).

Yes, as Christians we know what it's like to be on fire. But we may also know what it's like to be burned out—uninspired, unenthused, and cold inside. I have known such times in my own life and ministry, days when I looked for that fire, but found only ashes inside, weeks when I sought even a flicker of light, but could see only darkness of heart, and the flame gone out. Perhaps you have known this experience as well. How hard it can be to keep serving in Jesus' name when it seems there's no energy left!

When these times of darkness come, we cannot re-ignite ourselves. We don't even have two sticks to rub together. But we need not be discouraged, for we know the eternal Fire Starter. We hear his words, spoken anew: "I come to bring fire," Jesus says, addressing us each by name, "and how I wish the blaze were ignited!"

Do you wish that as well? How intent are you to see that fire rekindled in your life? How eager are you to see your church aflame with love for Jesus Christ? This desire is holy desire, too. But no matter how much we want renewed zeal, it cannot match his desire that we should have it. Our longing to be rekindled will never reach the magnitude of his longing to see it done. This is, after all, the mission of Jesus. It's his purpose; it's what he's about. If we hang around with him, sooner or later we'll go up in flames. And those around us will see the light and feel the warmth. And those we serve will catch that fire, too.

Questions for reflection

1. When you think of fire, what associations come to your mind? Can you think of other ways that fire is used as an image in the Bible, in addition to the ones mentioned in this chapter?

2. We're all familiar with icons depicting Jesus as the good shepherd, or Jesus as teacher. If you were to paint an icon of Jesus as a fire starter, what would it look like? How might you symbolize in the painting some of the different aspects of his fire that this chapter talks about?

3. Have you experienced the fire that Jesus brings as a purifying fire? Give some examples from your own life.

4. "Yes, as Christians we know what it's like to be on fire. But we may also know what it's like to be burned out—uninspired, unenthused, and cold inside." Share your own experiences of being on fire, or feeling burned out. If you felt burned out at any time in your life, how did you get through it?

5. What does a church that's "on fire" look like compared to a church that's not? What can individual believers in any congregation do to help keep the fire burning?

Seven

Encountering
Jesus in Prayer

Reading the spiritual thoughts and experiences of brothers and sisters in Christ can be very nourishing for all of us, as it enables us to taste the divine goodness in the lives of others, and so can lead us closer to God. But as the townspeople of Samaria discovered, it's one thing to believe because of what we are told, and quite another to spend time with Christ ourselves, and to know with the conviction of our own experience that "this is truly the Savior of the world" (John 4:39–42).

Here follow six meditations that may facilitate spending time with Jesus. The first two are based on biblical texts; the remaining four are imagery meditations. They are in no particular order, and are not linked thematically to previous chapters in the book. They can be used for either individual prayer or group prayer.

In the latter case, it's best for a prayer leader to read through the meditation in advance so as to be familiar with its contents and flow. The leader invites the participants to close their eyes, and turn their attention to the presence of God, and the presence of the risen Jesus Christ. Be sure to give enough time at this point for everyone to quiet down and become centered. Then proceed with the meditation, reading slowly and contemplatively, and pausing where indicated. Don't rush these moments of pause, as they are most often the times of greatest intimacy with God.

Let the people come out of the meditation slowly. Then it's always a good idea to invite the group to share what happened in their prayer, to the degree that they feel comfortable. No one should feel any pressure to share, nor should anyone attempt to judge or interpret another's experience.

When using these meditations for personal prayer, it will be necessary to keep the book at hand. Choose a quiet place, if possible, and then proceed at your own pace, but again, without hurry. Give yourself—and Jesus—the luxury of quality time spent together.

1. Called by the Lord

This meditation is based on John 1:35–41. It invites you to enter into a personal dialogue with the Lord about your own vocation as a disciple.

John the Baptist is standing with his disciples. He had earlier been speaking of Jesus, giving testimony publicly that Jesus was the Lamb of God, the anointed one, the chosen one. Now in verses 35–36 we read:

> The next day John again was standing with two of his disciples, and as he watched Jesus walk by, he exclaimed, "Look, here is the Lamb of God!" The two disciples heard him say this, and they followed Jesus.

Thus Jesus' first disciples follow Jesus because of the faith testimony of another person. All of us have likewise set out on the path of Christian discipleship because of the faith testimony of others—because we have heard the good news of Jesus proclaimed.

Who were the witnesses to Jesus in your life? Who pointed you to the Lord of Life? Remember these people—speak to the Lord about them with gratitude. (*Pause*)

The gospel text continues:

> When Jesus turned and saw them following, he said to them, "What are you looking for?"

See how the Lord takes the initiative in establishing relationship with his would-be disciples. His words, "What are you looking for?" are the first recorded words of Jesus in the gospel of John. They are words Jesus addresses to all who would follow him—they are words Jesus addresses to you.

What do you want from Jesus? Why do you follow him? What are the desires of your heart that have set you upon the

Way of Christ? Jesus asks you "What are you looking for?" Answer him in prayer.

The gospel text continues:

> They said to him, "Rabbi," (which translated means Teacher), "where are you staying?" He said to them, "Come and see." They came and saw where he was staying, and they remained with him that day.

Those first disciples asked Jesus where he lived, and Jesus, by inviting them to his home, brought them into personal relationship with himself.

But in the richness of John's gospel, this simple dialogue has even deeper spiritual significance. For, as the first disciples would learn, the real dwelling place of Jesus is in the Father. To "come and see" where Jesus stays is to enter into the mystery of his divine identity.

You have received Jesus' invitation to come and see. You have been called to know Jesus in a relationship of personal intimacy, and to follow him as his disciple. Spend some time renewing your response to Jesus' invitation. In your own heartfelt words, commit yourself to following him. Ask him to help you see more clearly what it means to be his disciple.

Further in the gospel we read of how Andrew, one of the first disciples of Jesus, spread the good news of his discovery:

> One of the two who heard John speak and followed him was Andrew, Simon Peter's brother. He first found his brother Simon and said to him, "We have found the Messiah" (which is translated Anointed). He brought Simon to Jesus, who looked at him and said, "You are Simon son of John. You are to be called Cephas" (which is translated Peter).

Andrew came to Jesus because of the testimony of John. Now, having found the Christ, he seeks to bring others into a personal contact with him. Thanks to Andrew's outreach, Simon Peter became a disciple of Jesus. With whom might you share Jesus? Whom does Jesus wish to call to discipleship through your witness?

When Jesus met Simon, he looked hard at him and gave him a new name. Jesus saw something in Simon, something that prompted him to call Simon "Rock." Jesus sees into your heart as well. Listen to Jesus now. He wants to tell you what he loves in you.

2. Healed by the Lord

Read Luke 5:17–26 slowly, prayerfully. Read through it several times. Now let the scene unfold before your inner eye. Imagine the scene in all its detail, from beginning to end—watch it as you would a movie.

Observe the expressions on the faces of the audience, the stretcher-bearers, the paralyzed man, and Jesus. Listen carefully to Jesus' words, and to the tone of his voice.

Does the scene stir any feelings or thoughts in you? Share them with Jesus in prayer.

Imagine the scene again, only this time you are the paralyzed one, lying on the stretcher. What is it like to be paralyzed like this—dependent on others for everything, unable to walk, or work, or make love?

Feel yourself being carried by your friends to the house, then up to the roof, then down through the roof to the presence of Jesus and the crowd. Look up from your stretcher into the faces of those standing on the roof, lowering you to the floor. Look up from your stretcher into the face of Jesus. What do you see in his face?

Listen to his words addressed to you, and experience the deep personal healing he gives you. Share your thoughts and feelings with Jesus in prayer.

All of us are paralyzed, in some way, on some level. Of what paralysis has Jesus already healed you? How are you still paralyzed? Reflect on these things, and talk to Jesus about them.

Who are the people in your life who have served as your stretcher-bearers, bringing you on different occasions to Jesus?

Think about these persons now, thank God for them, and pray for them.

Imagine the scene again, only this time you are one of the stretcher-bearers, bringing a paralyzed person to Jesus. Who is the person lying on the stretcher? Who are the others who carry the stretcher with you? What do you see in the face of Jesus as he looks up to you on the roof of the house?

See Jesus give deep healing to the one you have brought to him. Share your thoughts and feelings with Jesus in prayer.

Who are the paralyzed people you know? Perhaps you are needed to serve as a stretcher-bearer. Ask Jesus how to do this, and for the courage and love to act as stretcher-bearer whenever someone is in need.

3. A Walk in the Woods

Imagine you are standing in the middle of a field
on a bright sunny day.
The sky over your head is deep blue
and there isn't a cloud in sight.

You feel the sun shining warm
on your face and shoulders.
You look to your left and see
wildflowers of every color and variety.
You look to your right and see wildflowers.
See how many of them you can identify. (*Pause*)

A gentle breeze is blowing
through the grasses of the field
and you hear the breeze
as it rustles through the grasses of the field,
and you feel the breeze
blowing soft against your cheek.
And the air is filled
with the sweet scent of wildflowers.
You hear the sound of the bees
buzzing about their work in the field.

You are standing alone
in the midst of this field of wildflowers
on this bright sunny day,
and your feet are upon a narrow, dusty path
that runs through the middle of the field.

You begin to walk down the path,
slowly at first, then more briskly.
Ahead of you, in the distance
is a forest of large pine, spruce, and evergreen trees.
And as you draw nearer to the forest
the grasses of the field become low scrub bushes.
You follow the path into the forest and pause.

The air is much cooler here,
and the narrow dusty path
has become soft and moist beneath your feet.
The floor of the forest is covered with brown pine needles,
and the air is filled with the scent of pine.

And you listen to the silence of the forest,
and as you listen, you hear, very faintly
the sound of hammering.
You hear the sound of hammering
coming from somewhere deep within the forest.
You begin to follow the path farther into the forest,
and as you walk, the sound of the hammering
grows louder and louder.

Soon you come to a clearing,
and there in the midst of the clearing
stands a small stone cottage with a black slate roof.
A large stone chimney is coming up one side of the cottage,
and a wisp of white smoke is coming
from the top of the chimney.
The cottage has simple pane glass windows;
beneath one of them someone has planted a garden.

It is obvious that the sound of the hammering
is coming from inside this cottage,
so you walk to the old heavy wooden door
and lift the round black iron knocker, and knock.
The sound of the hammering ceases,
and you hear footsteps coming to the door.

The door opens, and there stands
a middle-aged man with dark hair and a beard.
He is wearing a leather work apron.
When he sees you he smiles and speaks your name, and says,
"I'm so glad that you are here. Come in."

You walk into the simple one-room cottage,
and look around at the rustic furniture.
There is a fire burning in the fireplace,
and near the fireplace is the carpenter's workbench.
The carpenter motions for you to sit down
on a low bench near the window.
For a few moments he resumes his work,
taking up a large plane
and running it across a piece of rough-cut pine,
the large wooden shavings falling to the floor beneath.
The room is filled with the smell of fresh wood,
and the carpenter is humming as he works.

Then the carpenter puts down his tool
and, wiping his hands on his apron,
he comes and sits beside you on the bench.
Once again he smiles and says,
"I'm so glad that you have come."

He says, "Tell me, what's in your heart right now?"
Answer him. (*Pause*)

The carpenter listens to you as you speak.
He listens from somewhere deep within himself.
And you know that you have never been
so completely listened to before.
And still the carpenter is listening to you. (*Pause*)

Then the carpenter says,
"I have something to tell you.
Something that's important for you to hear right now,
at this point in your life."
And he leans close to your ear and whispers.
Listen! (*Pause*)

Have you anything you wish to say
in response to the carpenter's words? (*Pause*)

Then the carpenter stands and says,
"I also have a gift for you,
something I want you to have right now."
And he walks to the mantel of the fireplace
and takes down a small wooden box,
which he brings and places in your hands.
Open it. (*Pause*)

Is there anything you wish to say
in response to this gift? (*Pause*)

Then you stand, and walk with the carpenter

to the door of the cottage.
You have only a few more moments with the carpenter.
Is there anything further you wish to tell him? (*Pause*)

Then the carpenter puts both of his hands on your shoulders,
and looks you full in the face and says,
"Know that I am with you, always."

You turn, and walk out of the cottage
and begin back down the path through the clearing,
holding in your hand the gift
which the carpenter has given you.
The door of the cottage closes behind you,
and the sounds of the woodworking resume.

Through the clearing you walk,
and back into the forest of pine and spruce and evergreen trees,
holding in your hand the gift that the carpenter has given you.

Through the forest you walk,
and back into the field of wildflowers.
And once again you feel the sun
shining warm on your face and shoulders,
you feel the breeze blowing soft against your cheek.
And you listen to the sounds of the breeze
rustling through the grasses of the field.

Spend a few moments now in quiet thanksgiving.

Open your eyes.
We conclude this meditation.

4. One Evening by the Lake

Imagine that you are sitting alone on a rock,
by the side of a small, quiet lake,
in the midst of a forest,
at evening time.

The setting sun is just dipping below the tops of the tall trees
on the opposite side of the lake,
and the blue sky is taking on deeper hues of purple and rose.
The water is smooth as glass,
disturbed but briefly here and there
by insects or creatures of the lake.

The trees are mirrored, clear and perfect,
in the smooth surface of the water.

You see the birds flying about in the treetops.
You hear them chirping and whistling
in one last burst of activity before nightfall.

The day's warmth is fading slightly now.
You feel the settling dampness in the air
as it grows cooler,
and with every breath you take in the rich smells of the forest.
And you are sitting alone upon the rock,
at the side of this quiet lake at dusk,
and you are feeling very much at peace.

Then, behind you, you hear the snap of a twig,
and you know that someone is there.
You turn and look,
and it is Jesus.

Without saying a word,
he sits down beside you at the edge of the lake,
and simply smiles at you.
And for a few moments you sit silently in his presence,
in the warmth of his gentle smile. (*Pause*)

Then Jesus speaks your name.
He says, "I have loved you with an everlasting love.
I want you to know that I am constant in my affection for you."
How do these words make you feel? Tell him. (*Pause*)

Then the Lord tells you how much he has cherished
the times of special intimacy that the two of you have shared.
You have indeed known times of felt closeness to Jesus,
perhaps through a sacrament, or through the Scriptures,
or when in prayer.

Remember now one of those special times.
What was it like? How did you feel then?
Share with Jesus the thoughts and feelings
that memory evokes. (*Pause*)

As you speak of these things,
you realize the many ways
in which he has been present in your life,
strengthening you, guiding you, nourishing you.
You are grateful,
yet you still hunger for more of Jesus.
Ask him how you might grow closer to him.
Listen to his response. (*Pause*)

You realize now that Jesus is about to depart.
You want to give him something before he goes,
some little thing that will express your gratitude,
something that will symbolize your gift of self to him.

On the ground at your side is a canvas bag
that you brought with you to the woods.
Inside that bag is the small gift
that symbolizes your devotion to him.
Reach inside, take out your gift, and give it to Jesus.
Be attentive to his reaction. (*Pause*)

Then, Jesus takes his leave,
and you are again alone on the rock
at the side of the quiet lake.
The sun has set, and the first stars are seen in the sky.

Spend a few moments in thanksgiving.

Open your eyes.
We conclude this meditation.

5. Early One Morning

Imagine that you are leaning against a large, cool rock
in an open garden.

It is very early.
The sun has just appeared over the horizon,
and you feel its first rays warm upon your face.
The birds are chirping in the trees
as they begin their day's activity,
and you listen to the sounds of the birds.

The morning air is clear and clean.
You take in the air in a slow, deep breath,
smelling its freshness, feeling its purity.

You see the dew glistening about your feet,
crystalline droplets,
shining silver upon the green grass.
Scattered amid the trees you see the daffodils,
proud of their springtime glory,
bright yellow and white.
You are at peace in this garden.
You are feeling thoroughly alive,
all your senses filled with the radiance of morning.

Off to your right you see an opening in the base of a hill,
and you begin to walk toward that dark opening.
You reach the cave, and peer in.
It is damp, cool,
and smelling of moss, and secret decay.

You remember the words of Scripture,
like a spoken voice they say:
"He is not there, He is risen
Seek not the living among the dead."

As you turn from that dark opening,
you see the Lord standing in the garden.
He is shining in the splendor of his resurrection,
perfected in the glory of the Father.
He is looking at you.
He is smiling.
Look at Jesus, look at his face.
Contemplate him in his resurrection. (*Pause*)

You see his arms are open.
His hands are beckoning.
Go, run to him now.
Speak to him of your joy.
Speak to him of your love.
Tell him your thanksgivings
for the good things of your life. (*Pause*)

Jesus wants to speak to you as well.
He wants to tell of his joy, his love.
He wants to thank you for responding to his call.
Listen to Jesus. (*Pause*)

Now someone else is coming to your mind,
someone who is in need of new life from Jesus,
someone who is trapped by the powers of death,
someone in need of good news.

Leave Jesus' side now and run and find that person.
Bring that person back with you to this garden,
to the arms of Jesus.
Watch what Jesus says and does. (*Pause*)

Now you are alone with Jesus again.
How good it is to be in his presence!
Though this special time of prayer must come to an end,
your awareness of his presence can grow to fill all your days.

Take a few moments to ask him for this grace,
to open to this grace,
then open your eyes.

6. The Cathedral

Imagine that it is a cold, late night in winter.
You are standing alone on a city street.
The city sounds have died down,
and all you hear is the sound of the wind blowing, blowing.
It is icy, crisp, biting,
fresh-smelling but harsh against your skin.
You wrap your coat more tightly around you,
and pull your collar up close about your face.

You are standing before a large, imposing church
built of massive gray stones,
a cathedral with towering steeples
and heavy, dark, wooden doors.
The large stained glass rose window above the central door
is aglow with light from within.
You climb the steps and approach the door,
hopeful that it is unlocked.
You take the handle and pull.
The door resists at first, but then swings open.

The warm dry air encloses you like a blanket,
and you proceed through the vestibule
onto the mosaic tiled floor of the cathedral.
The cathedral is filled with light,
adorned with colors and paintings,
and smelling of incense and candle wax.
Take a few moments to look around the cathedral.
Let it fill your senses with its ancient beauty. (*Pause*)

As you look around you see no one else in the cathedral.
No one is kneeling before the tabernacle,
no one is waiting at the sacristy door.
There is no janitor sweeping the floor,
no sacristan cleaning the altar.
It is silent, silent in the cathedral;
you stand in the aisle alone,
and you listen to the silence.

But wait—
out of the corner of your eye you catch a faint movement,
a huddled figure in a side pew,
sitting, but with head bowed.
Asleep, or praying?
You watch him in the silence, your heart pounding.
Could it be? Could it be?

Walk to the man sitting in that side pew.
He is the reason you have come to this place.
As you draw near to him, he lifts his face.
Sit down at his side, let him take your hand.
Listen to him…he is speaking. (*Pause*)

You have known his call to service.
Share with him now your frustrations and fears.
Tell him of your joys and sorrows in your labors for love of him.
Then listen again to his words of wisdom. (*Pause*)

What is your biggest need right now?
What is the request that surfaces from your heart?
Tell it to him. (*Pause*)

What peace you know, there at his side!
But he is getting up.
He smiles at you, and gets up.
Without a word of goodbye,
he walks past you and heads down the aisle.
Without a word of goodbye,
he has disappeared through the cathedral doors.

Get up now. Go after him.

Appendix
Tips for Small Group Study

The Ongoing Work of Jesus: His Mission in Our Lives is ideal for small group study and discussion. Typically, a discussion group based on this book would meet for six sessions, covering one chapter in each session.

Group leaders do not need an extensive theological background to facilitate the study. A general pastoral sensitivity to others, coupled with an ability to deal with group dynamics, will suffice. I recommend that leaders read the entire book through before the first session so that they have a clear idea of its message and approach.

The six prayer exercises in chapter seven can be used for group meditation. Starting each meeting with one of these prayer exercises is a great way to help people "shift gears" from the busyness of the day, and center themselves on the presence of Christ in their midst. Make sure to allow time for participants to share their experience with the meditation before beginning discussion of the assigned chapter.

It's always a good idea in a discussion group like this to

spend time at the start getting acquainted, with each one telling what he or she hopes to receive from participation in this study. A mutual commitment to confidentiality should be agreed upon at the start as well, which frees participants to talk more openly and helps build trust.

Let the Spirit lead!

Of Related Interest

Spiritual Surrender
Yielding Yourself to a Loving God
James A. Krisher

The author asserts that surrender is the fundamental life stance that strengthens all our choices. He focuses on surrender as a choice we make repeatedly no matter what the circumstance: in suffering, pleasure, joy, or prayer.
0-89622-721-9, 104 pp, $9.95 (M-94)

A Handful of Fire
Praying Contemplatively with Scripture
Sr. Carole Marie Kelly

Sr. Kelly draws the reader into an immediate relationship with the scriptural Word by introducing various methods of approaching a scriptural text. She offers help to see beyond what is familiar in a passage, and she explores sacred Scripture by focusing on the experience of Bible men and women who encountered God in life-changing ways.
1-58595-126-9, 192 pp, $12.95 (J-78)

The Yellow Brick Road
A Storyteller's Approach to the Spiritual Journey
William J. Bausch

Enter the world of Dorothy, Auntie Em, the Cowardly Lion, the Tin Man, and all the memorable characters from Kansas and Oz. With these classic figures, the author uses a treasury of stories and experiences to reveal the many roads that lead to prayer.
0-89622-991-2, 320 pp, $14.95 (J-35)

Available at religious bookstores or from:

TWENTY-THIRD PUBLICATIONS
A Division of Bayard PO BOX 180 · MYSTIC, CT 06355
1-800-321-0411 · FAX: 1-800-572-0788 · E-MAIL: ttpubs@aol.com
www.twentythirdpublications.com
Call for a free catalog